THE DILEMMA OF
RELIGIOUS KNOWLEDGE

E.T.S.U, AT TEXARKANA LIBRARY

022893

THE DILEMMA

OF

RELIGIOUS KNOWLEDGE

BY

CHARLES A. BENNETT

Formerly Professor of Philosophy in Yale University

EDITED, WITH A PREFACE, BY
WILLIAM ERNEST HOCKING

Alford Professor of Natural Religion, Moral Philosophy,
and Civil Polity in Harvard University

KENNIKAT PRESS/PORT WASHINGTON, N. Y.

THE DILEMMA OF RELIGIOUS KNOWLEDGE

First published 1931
Reissued in 1969 by Kennikat Press
Library of Congress Catalog Card No: 71-85986
SBN 8046-0538-6

Manufactured by Taylor Publishing Company   Dallas, Texas

ESSAY AND GENERAL LITERATURE INDEX REPRINT SERIES

PREFACE

CHARLES BENNETT was such a person as one would choose to be one's guide in thinking about religion. He had the great qualities, but also the graces, for that function. He was in the first instance a thinker who could *see,* and with an incorruptible veracity in telling what he saw. But there was also a tang and wit in the turn of his mind which saves him from heaviness in dealing with the most important of human concerns. His infinitely careful severing of error from truth, his merciless critique of the frivolities of professedly learned theories of religion, is all accomplished with a poet's sensitiveness of mental motion; and we are carried through the fallacies and into the depths without the noisy jar of dialectical machinery.

No sort of thinking in our time is so full of evasion as religious thinking. The masculine reflection which made the old theologies had at least this merit: It sought direct answers to the grave questions of human destiny, Does the conscious self survive death? Is there a strain of justice in the flow of the world? Is there a God who cares about persons and their rightness? Today, the difficulties of establishing such answers has concentrated attention on the prior question, *How can we know?* And to cover up that failure of nerve on this point which has been called agnosticism, sophisticated thinkers are inclined to dodge the dilemma by eliminating the "metaphysical" or "supernatural" from religion, and retranslating all its language so that it will apply only to what we suppose we *can* know—human affairs and the human mind.

So religion takes the form of "humanism," a cult of social and individual ideals, with no God unless it be humanity itself or the spirit of the tribe. Or it takes the form of a psychological self-discipline; or of a poetic and imaginative rendering of the human lot.

These evasions are the *motifs* which shape the course of Bennett's argument in this book. His conviction is, and he carries his point, that all such naturalizings of religion denature it and lose its essence. They would turn religious language into a metaphor, an analogy: but they are themselves mere analogies of religion. Like all similitudes, they add something to our knowledge of the thing itself: religion must be profoundly rooted in life in order to send its analogies throughout the structure of its great departments. But when the resemblance is taken for the substance of the original fact, it loses its own savor and stultifies the mind that accepts the substitution. Yet every well-worked-out theory of this sort gains a hearing in proportion to its author's ingenuity and to the widespread flabbiness among readers of that sense for realities which demands straight thinking. An honorable and courageous scent for the authentic is required to steer a true course.

In the nature of the case, the argument of this book is a series of rejections of illusory solutions of the problem of religious knowledge. Its manner, therefore, is necessarily negative; but no one will consider its outcome negative, unless to be liberated from a nest of plausible and widespread fallacies, and to be set on the way to the substance of the case, is a negative result. What Bennett positively puts into our hands as a cognitive compass is what I should call a doctrine of intuition; or, in his own language, an assertion of the

kinship between religious and poetic inspiration. This doctrine is brought to expression in a recent article on "Poetic
Imagination and Philosophy," for which he had an alter-
native title, "Poetic Imagination and Religious Insight." It
will be evident throughout that the artist in Bennett is a stay
and enlightenment to his religious sense. His indignation
against those who deny that art is "serious" makes him likewise indignant against those who, like Santayana, regarding
religion as a form of poetry, imply that religion is a form
of illusion.

Bennett is too eminently sincere a writer to pretend a
finality of result which he has not attained. This trait confirms our confidence in his leading: it is just such critical
and self-critical thought that is required to lay the foundation for an enduring philosophical achievement. Of this
metaphysical structure, he had made a beginning. The present volume represents the first part of a work whose second
part is entitled, in a draft outline, "The Metaphysical Problems of Religion." These chapters are, substantially, in the
form used at the time of their delivery in Boston. Professor
Bennett had intended to publish them in a much more elaborated form, and much of his material is in hand. It has been
deemed better, however, to abide by the text which he used
in lecturing. Chapters of this second part exist in rough
draft; and there are fragments of other chapters; but nothing here is finished.

The theme of these present pages, then, is the problem
of knowledge; nevertheless, their incidental discussions cover
the entire field of the philosophy of religion; for to a richly
furnished mind all the great topics of religion are involved in
the problem of knowledge. Thus we find Bennett discoursing

on immortality, on the proofs of God's existence, on miracle, prophecy, prayer and the cult, on revelation, on the wrath of God. And what he touches, he illuminates and deepens.

THE chapters of this volume had been given as a series of Lowell Lectures in King's Chapel, Boston, during the spring of 1930. They had been written out and revised. In bringing these materials together, I have made slight changes of wording, chiefly at the beginnings and endings of chapters, and of division, in order to drop the lecture form, and to give the whole its intended unity.

Bennett's hand could he have brought them to his own standard would have given these pages a poignant felicity of phrasing which my own editing lacks.

LET me now say a word about the philosophical career and outlook of my friend. A native of Ireland, he came to this country in 1909 after preparatory work at Trent College, Derbyshire, and after five years at Queen's College, Oxford, well grounded in the classical and literary discipline of "Greats," which carries with it a broad outlook in philosophy. Josiah Royce was at that time making weekly visits to Yale and lecturing in philosophy of religion and in ethics. Bennett was deeply stirred by his teaching; and remained to take his doctor's degree at Yale. Here I met him, first as a student and later as a colleague. His power and literary skill made him quickly salient. We desired him as assistant and instructor; and he continued to teach at Yale, through all the grades of academic promotion, until his death at the early age of forty-four on May 1, 1930.

In spite of the ill health with which he had to wage an

almost uninterrupted fight, he was a notably successful teacher, attracting large bodies of students to his general courses in ethics and philosophy of religion, and luring many to graduate studies in philosophy, particularly in his seminar on Mysticism. He had the academic virtues; but he had, besides, a candor, simplicity, and a quality of immediate personal concern for his problem, that drew all the sting of the academic from his discourse. He was genial in his relations with students: he enjoyed teaching, and they enjoyed being taught. In such relationships, eternity is present: there is no need of hurrying on to something else; no unhappy pressure of the unfinished topic; but thought is alive, and the mind expands without realizing the energy it is putting forth. Knowing his personal suffering, it is remarkable that none of his friends could think of Bennett as other than a happy man. His humor, his constant play of thought in letters and in conversation, were those of a spirit not merely reconciled with its world, but delighting in it. I do not say that Bennett was free from moments of depression. But I do say that the impression of his life is that of one who realized to the full the flavor of successful living in his professional, his domestic, and his social life.

The literary output of such men is often limited in quantity, for the reason that written expression may seem to them less necessary, or at any rate, less urgent. They communicate themselves without the indirection of manuscript and print. And I think that Bennett would have been content to allow his printed output in philosophy to grow slowly even had his physique permitted more constant labor. He has one book, an essay; but that book is masterly, both in thought and in literary quality. And he has a number of philosophical articles and reviews, of which I give a partial list.

Articles

1. An Approach to Mysticism.
   Philosophical Review, 27: 392.
2. Art as an Antidote for Morality.
   International Journal of Ethics, 30: 160.
3. Bergson's Doctrine of Intuition.
   Philosophical Review, 25: 45.
4. Religion and the Idea of the Holy.
   Journal of Philosophy, 23: 460.
5. Poetic Imagination and Philosophy.
   Yale Review, Winter, 1931.

Reviews

1. The Meaning of God in Human Experience, by W. E. Hocking.
   New York *Times*, December, 1912.
2. English Philosophers and Schools, by James Seth.
   Journal of Philosophy, 10: 53.
3. Race Questions and Other American Problems, by Josiah Royce.
   Philosophical Review, 20: 75.
4. The Relation of John Locke to English Deism, by S. G. Hefelbower.
   Philosophical Review, 28: 423.
5. Volonté et conscience, by P. Frutiger.
   Philosophical Review, 31: 86.

Perhaps it was not for him to realize how much his type of thought was needed. He had that which our current temper lacks, and which many of our critics also lack: joy, vision, reverence, a true perception of beauty. But while we cannot prevent the running out of our minds to what he might have done had he not been cut off in the maturity of his powers, we may also remember that the working of such a quality as his is like the working of an enzyme. It need not be so much in itself, for it multiplies its effect, and pervades the community of thought, and endures.

WILLIAM ERNEST HOCKING

Harvard University,
    January, 1931.

CONTENTS

022893

0244171

CHAPTER I

RELIGION AND THE SUPERNATURAL

ATTEMPTS to define religion have been notoriously unsatisfactory. It is too complex in constitution, too diverse in its manifestations, too deeply colored by personal emotion, for any summary rendering of its essence. Such riches, we feel, can hardly be compressed within the limits of a formula. Yet anyone who has reflected upon religion, however reluctant he may be to define it, must have formed some idea of what is most characteristic and important about it. It may be the belief in God, or the influx of moral energy, or the sense of sin, or the institution of the cult, but, however it be named, there will be some permanent element in the total meaning which identifies though it does not exhaust it. I propose to begin these inquiries, therefore, by disengaging what seems to me this central and all-important thing in religion. I shall try to evoke in your minds some general idea of what I mean by religion. Then I shall be in a position to explain the particular form which I wish to give to the problem of religious knowledge.

Let us begin with an experiment. Pragmatism tells us that the nature of a thing is revealed by the difference it makes. Let us look for light on religion by subtracting it, in imagination, from life, and observing what difference is made. How should we describe the climate of the irreligious or the nonreligious mind? Let us look at a specimen.

I am thinking of a man of about forty-five, healthy, fairly successful, reasonably happy, a "hard" business man. It is the hardness that strikes you most of all. One cannot call him deliberately selfish, for one never discerns any sign of a struggle between his egoism and any altruistic impulse, but he is selfish in the sense that the claims of others simply do not exist for him. Having defined his goal he makes for it straight as a Roman road, indifferent to the damage he does on the way. You see a mixture of unscrupulousness and cruelty, but he is cruel, in the words of one of Mark Rutherford's characters, "not with the ferocity of the tiger, but with the dull insensibility of the cart-wheel." Inaccessible to the influence of the normal human sentiments, he is naturally insensitive to music or to poetry. If he ever considered them at all he would dismiss them as so much idle vaporing. He is interested in pictures and books, but only for their commercial value. He is not purblind to natural beauty, but a mountain is a mountain and a flower a flower, nothing to rave about, you understand. He takes physical exercise and keeps fit, enjoys a good meal and a good cigar. As for religion in the strict sense, I suppose that such ideas as God, a future life, redemption, have never even been candidates for his consideration. It is so obvious to him that this visible tangible world is the only one that can or need be taken into account. In sum, not an immoral man, not a "blasphemer," nor even a man who is not often good company. No, if he frightens me, as he sometimes does, it is not because of any positive force of evil in him, but because of something he lacks. What is it? How shall I name it? His world, I think, is terrifyingly hard and bright. "Things are what they are," and their individual shapes are clear-cut, with no saving mistiness of outline. There are no ghosts there to communicate the thrill of mystery or the shudder of awe. That world, like its separate contents, stands self-explanatory and self-sufficient, suggesting nothing beyond itself. And the mind which sees it is like the thing seen: there is no twilight in it.

The same might be said of another world where religion has no place, that of contemporary naturalism. This is again a world of bare facts with no crepuscular softening of contours, but facts of a different and more rigidly conceived order. The dogma of naturalism, that type of philosophy according to which all the data necessary for an account of the universe are to be found in the natural sciences, might be put thus: Only that which is measurable is real. That quantitative ideal has not yet been reached, but it marks the direction in which the sciences are moving. "If all the arts," says Santayana, "aspire to the condition of music, all the sciences aspire to the condition of mathematics." Naturalism assumes as a *fait accompli* what for science is only a hope or a premonition. The stages in the evolution of that conclusion are readily set down. The first step is to reduce religion, art, and morals, to psychology. The second, to reduce psychology to biology and physiology. The next, to reduce these to chemistry and physics. Whether you stop short at physics or let it evaporate into mathematics, whether you stop with atoms and the void, electrons, space-time, or "a dance of differential equations gone mad," will make little difference: in the long run mechanical forces, as being the only *verae causae,* will be all one need take account of: they determine what shall appear either in "the world of description or in the world of appreciation." Plainly, in such a world the hard physical facts are the only facts we can believe in or trust to. Mystical intuition, intimations of immortality, the voice of conscience, romantic love, beauty "daemonic," tranquilizing, or disturbing, none of these contain any report of a far country. They are projections from the brain, poetic additions to the real truth of things. *Flammantia moenia mundi* forsooth! Medieval ignorance that! Have not our explorers been to the rim of the world and brought back word that there is simply more of the same? Have we not discovered our boundaries and drawn our maps?

I shall not ask what is our considered criticism, but merely what is our impression of this world. If we rebel against it, as I think we do rebel, it is not because of violence done to the values of art, morality, and the rest, but because of a vague feeling that this scene is too brightly lighted, that the music of *this* sphere is without overtones. In the concrete world of experience with which we are familiar things come to us fraught with meanings; there is always more in them than we can express or define; they hint at some world beyond themselves from which they draw their life. Naturalism will not allow us to indulge these fancies. It is the incurable romantic in us that the naturalistic philosopher offends. Or, to put the same thing in another way, he has taken too literally that command, "Son of man, stand upon thy feet."[1] He moves overconfidently in a world too well known. We watch him, his head erect, secure in what he calls his scientific knowledge, and surely it is something more than an old atavistic fear of the jealous gods that makes us tremble for him. Does he, we ask, draw the line, the line of some τέμενος anywhere? Does he know the meaning of "Hitherto shalt thou come, but no further, and here shall thy proud waves be stayed"? Is there any fact before which he will bow the head as being too wonderful for him? Is there any spot the influence of which can impose silence for a moment on that confident, garrulous, explanatory tongue, about which he may exclaim, "Surely the Lord is in this place; and I knew it not"?[2] "Superstitious nonsense!" he will fling at us. Upon which we remark, "What you lack is religion." A comment, be it observed, and not a reply. But it is sufficient for our present purpose.

That missing element we are in search of may come nearer recognition if we look for a moment at the familiar contrast between magic and religion. We do not propose to enter upon any discussion of the problems about their relationship. Whether religion preceded magic or *vice versa,* whether magic is better regarded as primitive science or degraded religion, are questions we need not consider. Our interpretation of magic may be as misguided as it is arbitrary, but that will not matter if it helps us to show what we mean

by religion. Magic then, I should maintain, carries us
a stage beyond naturalism. Naturalism is supremely
confident, because it has made a clean sweep of supernature. It is "positivist," and deals only with that
which is clearly known. Magic retains a belief in the
invisible powers and is even more confident than naturalism. Underlying both is a desire to bend nature to
the purposes of man; but while the naturalist believes
himself to be engaged with impersonal forces which
he may legitimately exploit, the magician is trying to
put constraint upon the gods. Religion knows that the
gods are not to be lightly approached. Prayer and
worship always exhibit a chastened mood, and with the
development of the cult the moral requirements for
worship become increasingly emphasized. Magic, on
the other hand, has never known or has forgotten this.
Magic is hot for results; it is the will to power in its
most ruthless form; even the gods are to be compelled,
no matter what the means. Naturalism lacks humility
because it has found nothing to reverence; magic is
aware of the divine, but is without humility even in
that presence. Here is the attitude which in more reflective ages has come to be variously called πλεονεξία,
ὕβρις, superbia, frowardness. From this point of view,
magic is more than irreligious: it is the very antithesis
of religion.

We have briefly reviewed three typical attitudes
toward experience which we may call Secularism,
Naturalism, Magic. From all three religion was ab-
sent. If we now try to summarize the result of our
experiment I should say that what all three lack is

the sense of mystery. The moment religion appears upon the scene man's universe becomes divided into two: the holy and the secular, the sacred and the profane, the visible and the invisible, that which is eternal and real over against that which is vain and transient. The sense of mystery, in its simplest definition, is the sense of the unseen order supervening upon, shining through, and transfiguring the seen. It is this that is here proposed as the central element in religion.

So far we have the merest outline. There are several important features that must be filled in if we are to have a recognizable picture.

In the first place, then, the mystery with which religion confronts man is not that of the Unknown or the Unknowable. It is not constituted by the fact that man has come to the end of his power of explanation, nor is it the problem of seeing how there can be two orders of reality and what their relation is. The presence of the mysterious evokes, not the constraint that goes with ignorance, nor even the terror of the unknown, but a feeling of self-depreciation, if not of actual self-condemnation. The profane or the natural desires are not merely checked, they are abashed and chastened. For the unseen world of religion is that upon which man's fate ultimately depends, and it is felt to impinge upon the destiny of the human soul. Something more is required of him than the explanations of theology or metaphysics, primitive or civilized, can afford. Reflection cannot allay the first aboriginal alarm. Man must square his account

with that unseen order. Hence the bewildering growth
of taboos, the elaboration of the cult, the multiplica-
tion of religious duties and observances, the often
frantic or brutal attempts to "get right with God."
All these point to some initial sense of wrongness or
alienation from the divine. And so when I talk of the
sense of mystery I mean a mystery that is capable of
evoking the feelings of humility and awe.

Second, the Mysterious Power, if that expression
may be allowed for the moment, is a being with whom
man can in principle be reconciled. The reconciliation
may be variously conceived: it may be that of subject
and king, offender and judge, child and father; it
may be the concord of the sacrificial meal, or the rap-
ture of mystical salvation. In any event ultimate harmony between man and the divine is taken to be possible. We are here insisting on one side of what we
may call the ambivalence of the religious mystery. As
Otto puts it, the numinous is not only daunting but
alluring, or, as it might be differently expressed, if
religious fear moves man to withdraw from God the
impulse of worship moves him to approach God.

Third, worship, I have just said, undertakes to
establish reconciliation or communion with God. Even
in its most spontaneous and lyrical forms worship is
never merely impulsive. It is social or sociable in its
intention. It expects to be heard. This is still more
conspicuously true of worship as deliberate, as organized in the cult. Petition, thanksgiving, adoration,
propitiation, sacrifice, all are addressed to a being
capable of understanding and accepting them. They

are not uttered into a void. It takes two minds to make communion. The mysterious power, if it be the power that religion is concerned with, must be conceived as personal, at least to this extent, that he can hear his worshipers.

Fourth, religion generates devotion. By this I mean no more at present than that I am unwilling to call any experience properly religious which leaves the springs of conduct wholly unaffected. According to the Platonic tradition in Greek thought, the all-important thing in life was the vision of the good and the beautiful: the vision of the ideal once attained could be trusted to transform the substance of conduct to its own image. So religion, as a vision of the holy, must engender its own loyalties: its ecstasies are destined to express themselves in deeds. Thus I do not think that religion either in its beginnings or in its later stages has been separable from morals. Where it has led to otherworldliness or to an actual hostility to human nature we should have to accuse it of aberrations from its normal meaning.

We may reinforce this contention by recalling that the complement to worship—man's approach to God— is prophecy and revelation, God's approach to man. We should be ignoring one-half of the picture if we omitted those phenomena in which the divine is supposed to enter the human scene: from apparitions, voices, intuitions, commands, through the sacred book or the sacred law, up to the consummation of some actual incarnation of the god himself. The invisible world, in short, is never wholly invisible: it constantly invades the visible order, and that order is proportionately altered.

Here then is religion with its other world, its mysterious invisible order. And the problem of religious knowledge in its simplest terms is this: Can this other world be said to be known at all, and, if so, how is it known?

The thing that strikes one most about the mystery of religion is that it is foreign to the native air of our minds, that it is opaque to human intelligence. It is certainly grasped, yet it is not understood; if it reveals itself, it also conceals itself from rational comprehension. There is little or nothing that we can say about it that will withstand logical scrutiny. In spite of all the efforts of theologian and philosopher, supernature refuses to be naturalized or rationalized. It is as though in religion we came upon some surd in experience, some nonrational factor; and more and more I find myself coming to sympathize with that paradoxical assertion of the mystic that if God is to be known he must be known in "a cloud of unknowing." I would accept the words of the French sociologist Durkheim when he writes:

This division of the world into two domains, the one containing all that is sacred, the other all that is profane, is the distinctive trait of religious thought. . . . There is nothing left to characterise the sacred in its relation to the profane except their heterogeneity. . . . This heterogeneity is absolute. In all the history of human thought there exists no other example of two things so profoundly differentiated or so radically opposed to one another.[3]

If we wish to elaborate this idea, note first the way in which the sacred everywhere is the "not to be lightly approached." The ark, the temple, the chancel, are hedged about against profanation. The medicine man, the prophet, the priest, are set apart. Again, those natural objects in which *mana* resides are filled with mysterious potency, "the power to blast or to bless." At a more reflective stage these sentiments get expressed in the idea of the remoteness of God. While the gods are still tied fast to natural objects, that remoteness has to be spatially rendered, but, as Hocking observes, as soon as man can think beyond the sky or the sun, then beyond sky or sun God goes. Even today it is interesting to see what a weight of mystical profundity is felt to inhere in expressions such as "behind," "beneath," "beyond," "above," as applied to the divine. Once religion has escaped from materialism and idolatry it seems as though God could not stop short of the ideal, the limit. When Mr. Alexander writes, "Deity is thus the next higher empirical quality to mind, which the universe is engaged in bringing to birth,"[4] is he not giving us a philosophical transcription of the ancient impulse? Theology rings the changes on God as incomprehensible, or God as a *deus absconditus*. "True gnosis," says a Sufi mystic, "is nearer to silence than to speech." There you have the ultimate confession that the mystery is ineffable. And the philosopher is compelled to admit that his descriptions of the divine are after all only figures of speech. "Omniscience, omnipotence, infinite goodness, eternity, . . . are . . ., as Hegel observed, the figurative disguises of a faith in something of a different order from man."[5] "The truly 'mysterious' object," writes Otto, "is beyond our apprehension and comprehension, not only because our knowledge has certain irremovable limits, but because in it we come upon something inherently 'wholly other,' whose kind and character are incommensurable with our own."[6]

Let me exhibit in more detail this idea of the incommensurability of the two orders, the natural and the supernatural, by means of a specific example. Consider that unique attainment which under the name of salvation religion offers to its followers. What salvation means varies from religion to religion, from age to age, and perhaps even from person to person: it depends not only on what man needs to be saved from (e.g., ignorance, illusion, suffering, sin, doubt, dissipation), but upon what man is to be saved *to* (e.g., insight, Nirvana, Heaven, eternal life). I shall make no attempt here to analyze a concept of such extraordinary complexity, but content myself with pointing out a nonrational element in it in all its forms. If, for example, salvation brings knowledge or insight or illumination, then it is clearly not knowledge of a kind that constitutes any addition to our scientific or philosophical stock. What the saved person knows is not anything that he or anyone else can translate into definite propositions: it defies rational expression. To one who does not participate in it the insight seems meaningless or illusory. If salvation means power, then neither in quality nor in mode of operation is it the power familiar to or coveted by the natural man. Magnify power as *he* understands it and you get *Wille zur Macht*—the very opposite of spiritual power. So far removed is one from the other that their respective champions regard each other as extolling not strength but weakness. The scandal of the Cross, we might say, is that the weak things of the world have become strong. That is also the scandal of the Superman. If salvation, again, means eternal life, then eternal life, while it includes immortality, includes more than that. It is something that need not wait on the future for its assurance, something that can be known as present fact. It is some well-founded union with the ultimate source of life which enables one to regard physical death as an unimportant incident. If salvation means security, then that security is compatible with everything that the natural man regards as danger. "In the world ye shall have tribulation. . . ." Finally, the happiness which salvation brings with it is no mere magnification of natural happiness. Indeed, it is absurd to use such a pale word as happiness to describe anything so vivid and intense. For what religion confers is *bliss,* bliss unspeakable. *Quae jubilatio!* It is a thing as lyrical in its proper expression as its sources are obscure. The transports of the mystic or of the converted are as unintelligible to the secular mind as the felicity of the lover to the unromantic.

Let me try to set down the total impression made upon me by these examples of the incommensurability of the natural and the supernatural. On the one hand, when we approach the supernatural from this side, with each path that we follow we find that the trail suddenly ends. We cannot by going forward enter the country beyond nor discern what is there. We can only say, "It lies over there—where this trail and the others would lead if they did not break off." On the other hand, it is not a completely unknown nor undiscovered land, for religion in its own miraculous way can set one down there. But this sojourn in the promised land puts some of its strangeness upon one and impairs one's powers of speech. The traveler emerges with a stammering tongue. To those who have not been there he can give no clear account of what he has seen. He breaks off in despair, exclaiming, "Words are futile." He cannot bridge the gulf. There seem to be two worlds, that of nature and that of supernature; we find ourselves alternately now in one, now in the other, but the transition in either direction eludes us. Religion can show us no road back and we, in spite of our efforts, can find no road thither from this side.

So far, the statement of our problem has been made to depend on the thesis that what I have called the sense of mystery is the central thing in religion. This may seem too precarious a basis. Let me therefore essay a quite different line of approach, and one perhaps more generally acceptable, by way of examining the nature of faith. For it is by faith that religion is supposed to lay hold on its peculiar verities.

CHAPTER II

FAITH

THERE is something distinctive in the way in which religion supposedly knows or apprehends its objects. This specific faculty, to set it apart from scientific knowledge and reason, has been traditionally called faith. It is faith that plumbs the mysteries; it is to the eye of faith that divine truth is revealed; it is faith that is the vehicle of prophetic premonitions about the destiny of man and the cosmos. If we are to appreciate the basis of religious confidence we must examine the nature of faith.

To even the most superficial regard, faith presents a puzzling union of certainty and uncertainty. On the one hand, it is a state of assurance that seems to the believer self-sufficient. On the other, it always in some sense goes beyond the evidence, and, as if aware of this weakness, seeks to provide itself with rational justification. Failing to find this, it falls back on its original inarticulate conviction. These statements call for explanation. Let me take first the aspect of certainty.

That faith means certainty may seem a truism upon which it is not worth while to insist. Yet a failure to recognize what should here be obvious marks some familiar treatments of the subject. There is, for example, that all-too-facile reconciliation of science and religion whose substance consists in the statement that all science, like religion, is ultimately based on faith, —for science cannot proceed without a faith in the uniformity of nature or the rationality of the universe. Adversity makes strange bedfellows, and in the common recognition of ultimate uncertainty the ancient antagonists are to compose their quarrel. But as a matter of fact the faith of science and the faith of religion have nothing in common. The principle of the uniformity of nature is conditional, not categorical: it is a working assumption, the truth of which is being continually verified. The belief in God is categorical, not conditional. To religion faith in God is not a hypothesis, but a fact of immediate intuitive conviction.

There is another rendering of faith, conceived in much the same spirit, which demands more serious consideration. I shall let one of its exponents speak for himself.

Over every aspect of human life there hangs the prospect of a possible better, inviting us to achieve it, but without proof that we shall succeed, or even that it is worth our while to make the attempt. The coward within us asks for proof; cries out that the venture is not safe, and summoning the will to disbelieve has no difficulty in finding reasons for rejecting the invitation. The hero, on the contrary, finds in the terms offered the exact conditions to which his nature is fitted to respond. He would rather create the proof of his own valour than have it for nothing at the outset. He is not dismayed at finding himself in a universe which puts him under no compulsion to believe in God, Freedom, Duty, and Immortality. As a free soul he prefers not to be compelled to believe in anything—for how then could he be free?

I will venture to suggest to anyone who is troubled by doubts about the reality of God, not to trust the fortunes of his faith too unreservedly to the field of mere argumentation. . . . I suggest further that the only final way of ascertaining whether or no such God exists is by experiment, standing or falling by the issue, and resorting to the methods of argumentation only to conform or elucidate the results so obtained. The experiment first, the argumentation second.

But of what nature is the experiment in question? I conceive it being made in the following manner: "I will base my life on the assumption that somewhere, in the height above or in the depth below, Power is waiting to back me up. That Power, if I find it, shall be my God."[1]

You will notice that in the last sentence Professor Jacks uses the word "assumption." That is where I take exception. The idea that in religion the will to believe has the final word cannot stand. I do not deny that religion can create the heroic temper of mind, sweeping aside fears and scruples and the cautious reservations of the calculating intellect, but its heroism is of the kind that builds on some prior conviction. And surely the most striking historic function of religion has been to lift men from doubt and perplexity to a region of assurance and serenity. If there is any anchorage for human emotions, any one goal for human ambition, any solid foundation for courage to build on, it is religion that has supplied these things. If anywhere we break through from illusion into reality , it is in religion that we do so, and any interpretation of faith which ignores or denies this is frankly preposterous.

In spite of our objections there is clearly some truth in the views to which we have referred. Faith has something experimental or adventurous about it, in the sense that it goes beyond, and sometimes even against, what the facts seem to warrant. The evidence of faith is that of "things not seen." It is a form of certainty, but not the certainty that rests on demonstration. Thus it is sometimes said that faith begins where proof leaves off and that the failure of demonstration is faith's opportunity. An example is found in the statement that the conflict between the several accounts in the Gospels of the Resurrection of Christ is providential, for if the evidence of the Resurrection had been indisputable there would have been no room for faith on that point. One may smile at the *naïveté* of this reasoning, but I think it rests on a sound principle. One cannot properly be said to have faith in matters of fact. One does not talk of having faith in the coronation of Queen Victoria, or in the Second Law of Thermodynamics. If the truths which religion claims to grasp could be explicitly formulated and established by reason as are these propositions, then religion would have passed over into history or science or philosophy. Its assertions might be true, yet, paradoxically, they would have lost their religious significance. In order to preserve its identity religion is forced to distinguish objects of faith from objects of proof.

Yet one cannot deny that this distinction is, from the point of view of religion itself, unsatisfactory and dangerous. A faith which consists in believing what you can't prove is not very different from superstition, and the apparent discrediting of its claim to literal truth is something which religion cannot tolerate. An indemonstrable assurance is a precarious assurance.

Confronted by this embarrassment religion throughout its history has constantly sought the stability which comes from discovering rational grounds for belief. Religion argues, explains, offers proofs. The vast accumulation of apologetic, theology, philosophy of religion, is sufficient evidence of the strength and persistence of this impulse. Yet an impartial estimate of the success of these attempts leads one to conclude that they would better not have been made. Religion does not fare well under the assaults of criticism. Some of its assertions prove to be manifestly untenable if regarded as contributions to history, science, or philosophy, and the rest turn out to be overbeliefs or symbolical expressions. When the utterances of faith have been stripped of these accretions and the core of literal truth in them extracted, that residuum turns out to be so meager and uninteresting that it could not form the basis of any religion. Religion then repents of its rashness and sounds a retreat. It falls back on dogma or inarticulate conviction. Religious truths, we are now told, are mysteries revealed only to the eye of faith, and faith is a form of intuitive knowledge which defies rational expression. The predicament of religious knowledge is precisely that described in the classical words of Augustine about the nature of time: "If no one asks me, I know: if I wish to explain it to one that asketh, I know not. . . ."[2] And this oscillation between dumb intuition and argument, between undemonstrated conviction and demonstrable certainty, constitutes the very essence of faith. "Faith," as one writer succinctly puts it, "claims theoretical validity for its object, and at the same time implies that the object cannot be rationally known."[3]

Thus our analysis of faith has led us to the same conclusion that we reached by our first line of approach, the examination of the sense of mystery in religion. I think it is clear that our study of the structure of faith has simply revealed on the side of form the same difficulty that we encountered when we studied the content of religious knowledge. We cannot do without the supernatural, yet we cannot do with it; it refuses to be rationalized. Faith grasps its supernatural object, but cannot comprehend it; tries to say what it means, and then denies that it means what it has said; asserts in one and the same breath that it is knowledge and that it is not knowledge.

> O world invisible, we view thee,
> O world intangible, we touch thee,
> O world unknowable, we know thee,
> Inapprehensible, we clutch thee!

Surely a strange embarrassment of the human mind! What are we to make of a knowledge, if indeed it be knowledge, so perplexed and insecure? There is the heart of our problem.

I have spoken so far in general terms. These are always unsatisfactory. I will try to make the issue more vivid and concrete by taking a particular illustration of the predicament of faith.

Historic religion has brought to men a conviction that they are immortal, a conviction, let us say, reached not by demonstration, but by faith. Now the question of immortality is, I take it, for religion, a question of fact. When one says that he believes in immortality he claims to be asserting literal truth. It is when we ask *what* literal truth religion is sure of that the difficulties begin. And my contention is that religion is unable to give any reply that will withstand critical examination. Its assertion means something, but *what* it means religion is unable to declare. I will give some reasons in support of this contention.

In order to keep our treatment within manageable bounds I shall arbitrarily limit the meaning of immortality to personal immortality. Even when thus restricted it is susceptible of a variety of interpretations. I maintain, however, that no matter how it is interpreted immortality must mean at least survival of bodily death. It may and should, I believe, mean more: I cannot see how it can mean less. But how are we to think of this future state?

Belief in immortality is more than the aversion of the living being to extinction. It is a *conscious* rejection of what death implies, a protest against the thought of death and the final victory of material forces. It is a refusal to believe that the promise inherent in love, friendship, or genius is to be deprived of fulfilment. Now if this postulate is to be satisfied, the next life must be sufficiently like this one to afford an opportunity for the continuous development of the powers, hopes, and ideals that we have now. A mo-

024417

ment's reflection shows that this is incredible. A writer of unmistakable genius who is just beginning to discover his powers and whose best work lies immediately ahead of him meets an untimely death. Outraged by the apparent injustice, we assert our conviction that he will "get another chance." But do we seriously believe that people will write poems or novels in Heaven? If so, Heaven will be little more than a perpetuation of earthly conditions. Yet that is not what Heaven means. Again: in Heaven we are to "knit severed friendships up." But an interval of twenty years (say) separates the deaths of two friends. May they not have changed "out of recognition" in the interval? If so, the hope of friendship has been frustrated; if not, Heaven will have left them largely unchanged. But then, once more, it will not be Heaven.

We might multiply examples, but even those we have given may have been sufficient to make some persons impatient. It is vain, we shall be told, to speculate upon the particular conditions of the future life, and not only vain, but unnecessary. Faith in God is all that matters. If one have that, one is content to leave all to Him in the assurance that our lives are in his hands. This is a solution as persuasive as it is simple, but unfortunately it has the result of reducing the substance of immortality to the vanishing point. To be certain that there is immortality, yet not to know *what* one is certain of hardly bespeaks a robust faith. And so we confront a dilemma: either the conditions of the next life are largely identical with the conditions of this one—and then Heaven becomes ridiculous; or the conditions of the next life are so unlike the conditions of this one that we can say nothing about them—and then Heaven becomes superfluous.

Perhaps there is a way out of the dilemma. If religious faith can be independent of any concrete description of the future life, why may it not be satisfied by some rendering of its conviction which involves no reference to the future at all? Perhaps the belief in a future life is merely a figurative way of expressing some deeper philosophical truth. Following this line of reflection, various attempts have been made to discover the truth symbolized by personal survival and to restate it in a way that is free from difficulty. Let us glance at two or three of these.

We sometimes hear it said of a work of art, "When lesser works have perished, this will continue to be enjoyed." And a "classic" is, by common consent, a work that will endure. But endurance by itself is not enough to constitute a classic. Works of art are not classics because they endure: we predict that they will endure because we believe them to be supreme in their kind. Our appeal to survival, therefore, is only a clumsy way of expressing our conviction of their value. May not the survival of the soul be an analogous form of expression? When religion declares for immortality, may it not be uttering its faith in the intrinsic worth of the soul and its aspirations, or, in technical terms, its faith in "the axiom of the conservation of value?"

Again, we may be told, from a different point of view, that eternal life does not mean endless duration throughout future time, but a certain quality of life

022893

that may be a present achievement. To understand this requires a brief explanation.

"Time," it has been said, "is the form of the will." Reverie over the past, speculation about the future, are symptoms of some dissatisfaction with the present. It is because the present does not wholly engage us, because it disappoints, perplexes, or dismays us, that we send our minds ranging backward or forward in time. In such hours the present may come to have chiefly a mediate value: it prophesies or brings nearer that future where we fain would be. But there is such a thing as finding the present completely absorbing, when we are not eager for the future, for no amount of time could add anything to the value of what we have now. This is "the moment made eternity." And we can imagine a condition of life such that we should be absorbed in each stage of experience as it came to us, finding there a sufficient occupation for our interest and our devotion. Nothing would be merely preparatory or instrumental. We should know neither romantic unrest, nor surfeit, nor monotony. We should be living whole-heartedly and continuously in the present. For such an experience the distinctions of past, present, and future would have lapsed: it might, therefore, be called "living eternal life in the midst of time." To the attainment of this, rather than of some problematic future career, religion might well be asked to bend its energies.

A third meaning of eternal is "timeless." To call anything timeless is to assert not that it persists perpetually unchanged, but that in relation to it temporal terms are irrelevant. Truth is timeless in this sense. The relation, for example, between the premises and the conclusion of a syllogism is one of logical, not temporal, priority. The premises are not first true, so as then to engender later another true proposition—the conclusion. None of the three propositions ever began to be true. If we say that none of them will ever cease to be true, that does not mean that they will keep on being true; it simply means that to talk of their losing truth is as inappropriate as to talk of their acquiring it. From this point of view eternal life for the human soul would not mean perpetual life, but a life vicariously eternal through participation in the supra-temporal order of truth.

In spite of the merits of these attempts to divorce the concept of eternal life from that of a future life, they are all open to one objection. They all leave one question unanswered. It may seem too naïve even to deserve consideration, yet it refuses to down. Suppose that some human being has led a life which in its purpose and quality would be called eternal in any of the senses distinguished above, then our question is, What becomes of him after death? Is he annihilated? Does he have merely an "immortality of influence"? Is he absorbed in some mystical fashion into the divine? or does his personal life continue? We shall be told, perhaps, that this is a question which properly belongs to science, for it is concerned with literal fact—like the date of the next eclipse, and that therefore it falls outside the province of religion which is supposed to deal with values and ideals. But here we reach a point where we find it impossible to separate so neatly value from fact, for here the former depends on the latter. If the good man who has "lived eternal life in the midst of time" dies when his body dies, then the universe is flagrantly convicted of "unfriendliness." The fate of the good man in the next world determines our judgment of the value of this one. In other words, the appeal to the future is more than a piece of convenient symbolism: it is *necessary* symbolism. And the necessity of the symbol ties it somewhere to literal truth.

Thus we are brought back to the original position, that in this matter of immortality religion cannot abandon its claim to literal truth. Yet, as we have seen, religion is unable to give any intelligible statement of what that literal truth is. And this, as I said, is only a particular instance of the general problem. Religion professes to apprehend the supernatural, yet can give no finally valid account of it; claims to possess truth, but in the next breath declares its truth to be inexpressible. It is then inevitable that these pretensions should become suspect. The question becomes urgent: Is religion a source of cognitive insight? To study some of the answers that are being given to this question today constitutes the task of the chapters that are to follow.

CHAPTER III

SYMBOLICAL THEORIES: FEUERBACH

LET me resume in a few words the statement of our problem as we have now reached it. Religion deals with the supernatural, which is claimed to be an objective reality; the supernatural, however, is mysterious,— it constitutes a sort of surd, a nonrational factor in experience. The human intellect seems beaten back in its effort to construe the meaning of divine things. Religion does not lack certainty: it is sure of God, sure of salvation, sure of immortality; yet when it tries to give a coherent interpretation of these things it has to confess failure. It lacks perfect expression or adequate proof. Faith goes beyond the evidence: it is prophecy or divination; it is a laying hold of truth in advance of demonstration. Yet, as "believing what you can't prove" seems an irrational procedure, faith is constantly seeking for rational support, and failing to find it. Thus the life of faith tends to oscillate between a dumb intuition and an articulate expression in neither of which the mind can rest.

Whichever way we look at the situation, a doubt arises. Here is religion, claiming insight, yet unable to put that insight into words—assured of some truth, yet of truth that turns out to be ineffable. Perhaps, then, religion is the victim of an illusion: perhaps "there is nothing there, after all." Religion esteems its truth to be all-important, and we are reluctant to

discard that estimate. But is there any valuable difference between ineffable truth and no truth? The issue
becomes clear: Is the so-called knowledge of religion
really entitled to the name?

There is one fairly promising way out of the difficulty. It has long had its advocates, and it commands
in recent years a widening attention. For we have become increasingly alive to the problems of language
as we pass from one sphere of experience to another.
Religion is forced to employ the speech of common
day; and if this language fails to fit, a stiff literalism
in judging it must be fatal to understanding. If we
cannot substantiate the statements of religion, perhaps that is because we take them in the wrong sense.
If religion denies that it means what it says, that
may be because it does not succeed in saying what it
means. This intimates the policy of the type of theory
I have in mind. It contends that the utterances of
religion are to be taken, not as literal statements, but
as figurative or poetic renderings of some underlying
philosophical truth. Religious knowledge, in a word,
is symbolical.

In advance of any detailed examination, this theory
sounds persuasive. Even to a superficial regard it is
clear that there is much metaphor and poetry mixed
in with religious doctrine. One can hardly maintain
that the story of the Garden of Eden, for example, is
intended as sober historical fact, or that the doctrines
of Heaven and Hell are meant to embody contributions
to cosmic geography. The whole Christian story of the
Fall and Salvation of Man is to be taken less as his-

torical narrative than as a dramatic account of the soul and its destiny. I do not wish to suggest for a moment that religion can dispense with the historical; but clearly the historical element is valued not so much for itself as for what it signifies. Not the story, but the meaning of the story, is what counts.

There are always those who think that when they have shown—as can so easily be shown—that religion is poor science or poor history, they have somehow discredited religion. And to take all the language of religion literally would force us to agree with them. But if we realize that the symbol is transitory while the thing symbolized is permanent, we shall avoid the mistake of thinking that religion is refuted, or so much as touched, by such facile criticism. We cannot reach the position of religion, much less attack it, until we understand the use of the symbols it employs. We can be sure, therefore, that a theory which would explain religious language as through-and-through symbolic would lead us, for a distance, at least, in the right direction. If such a theory proves to be in error, it will be erring on the right side.

To say that religion speaks darkly, through figures or symbols, does not of itself afford much relief to the dilemma of religious knowledge. One must be endowed with the "ear to hear"; that is, he must have the key to the interpretation of the myth or parable. The symbolical theories we are about to consider profess to supply such a key, and thereby to bring religious assertions within the region of verifiable or testable statement. As our first representative exponent of this theory, it will be of advantage in many ways to choose a writer somewhat removed in time from the field of present controversy. I choose for this purpose the German philosopher, Feuerbach, who is not often referred to in this connection. I do this partly because his ideas have an intrinsic importance of their own, partly because, although the work on which my account is based, his *Das Wesen des Christenthums*, appeared as long ago as 1841, he anticipates in an interesting way many tendencies in contemporary thought about religion.

In any general classification Feuerbach's teaching would be described as positivist or humanist. We must therefore begin with his account of human nature. The defining characteristic of man is self-consciousness. Man differs from the animals in that he distinguishes himself from nature and from other animal species. He knows himself as man. We might express this by saying that man is the only species, so far as we know, that has produced sciences—biology, anthropology, and so forth—which have the nature of the species as their subject matter. Birds, presumably, do not have a system of ornithology, and dogs are innocent of cynology.

This self-consciousness means that any given man is a twofold being: he is at once this particular man and man universal. He is limited by his special position in place and time, and by his individual peculiarities, but he is unlimited in that he is aware of, and can express, his humanity. The capacity for self-transcendence ap-

pears conspicuously in the ideal of disinterested knowledge (or science) on the one hand, and in the ideal of
disinterested conduct (or morality) on the other. The
aim of science is the dispassionate, impersonal acknowl-
edgment of fact. The seeker after truth must try to
divest himself of his personal desires and emotions; he
must discount the influence of whatever is peculiar to
his private perspective. To say, "This is true," is to
say, "Any other mind in my position would give the
same report"; it is to claim to represent the ideal human observer. In the same way, the moral man is he
who renounces all selfish pursuits and narrow ends,
and is moved to action by the sheer claim of the ideal—
justice or truthfulness, or whatever it may be. He is
the man of principle, the impartial man. He surveys
the issues of conduct not merely through his own
eyes, but through the eyes of all humanity.

So far we are on ground that Kant and Hegel have
made familiar. But now Feuerbach introduces a doctrine peculiar to himself. We have said that the individual man is aware of his finite limits. He must
therefore be more than finite, for, according to the
Hegelian principle, accepted by Feuerbach, he who
recognizes a limit is already in reflection beyond it.
What does this imply? The Hegelian answers: It
implies that man is part of an Infinite Being. Feuerbach will have none of this. He says it implies that
man is part of Humanity, that the stirrings of the so-
called Infinite in him are the stirrings of Humanity.
The idea that beyond Humanity there is anything is
an illusion. What theology and philosophy mistake

for the Infinite or the Absolute is nothing but man's "latent nature."

His reasons for this conclusion are what concerns us here, for it is on this that his entire doctrine rests. In brief, his position depends on what has always been the stronghold of subjective idealism.

> Man [he writes] cannot get beyond his true nature. He may indeed by means of the imagination conceive individuals of a so-called higher kind, but he can never get loose from his species, his nature. . . . A being's understanding is its sphere of vision. As far as thou seest, so far extends thy nature; and conversely.[1]

This idea can be illustrated on every hand. We perceive in any object only what interest and education enable us to discern there. To the geologist the rock masses tell a story; to others they are merely nature's *débris*. The callous man is blind to suffering, and, while we may deplore his lack of sensibility, we can hardly blame him for it, for it is unreasonable to expect him to transcend his own insight, feeble though that may be. From a naturally dull or untrained ear are concealed those beauties of music that are evident to a cultivated musical taste. In general we may say that the mind can know only what its own nature reveals. The unknown must be reduced to terms of the known before it can be assimilated. The mind could never know anything that was incommensurate with its native powers. We know what we are.

From this Feuerbach draws the astounding conclusion that we know only what we are: that the so-called objective world is merely the mind externalized. In his own words, "The object of any subject is nothing else than the subject's own nature taken objectively."[2] I say astounding, because the inference runs thus: We know *with* idea, therefore we can know only idea. This is a plain *non sequitur*. The facts might be exactly as Feuerbach describes them, yet it might still be true that ideas reach reality and that we can have valid knowledge of that which is other than idea. If he fails to see this, it is, I believe, because he entertains an erroneous notion of the function of an idea: he is haunted by a ghost which philosophy has not yet succeeded in laying. Ideas, he seems to think, interpose a limiting medium between the mind and its object: they are, as it were, colored glasses which prevent us from seeing the object as it is in itself. Yet, on the other hand, we cannot know without ideas; the mind, in terms of our figure, cannot remove its colored glasses. Hence, from Feuerbach's point of view, the ambition to know the object "as it really is in itself" implies mental suicide—the self-contradictory ideal of knowing the object by destroying the means of knowing. But if we assume, as we must assume, that the mind from the outset of its career is in direct contact with reality, we can avoid Feuerbach's subjectivism.

This is a subjectivism of Humanity, of man universal, of the species, and not of the individual man. The limits of the individual are not final: he can and does transcend them, as we have seen, in science, in philosophy, and in the moral and aesthetic judgments. He can do this because he belongs to Humanity, and the powers of Human Nature are his. But Humanity cannot transcend itself. Beyond Humanity we cannot go. Humanity is the Absolute. To talk of God, the Infinite, the Most Perfect, is not to refer to some superhuman being, but merely to exhibit man's farthest reach, his idea of Humanity's best.

That which is to man the self-existent, the highest being, to which he can conceive nothing higher—that is to him the Divine Being. . . . If God were an object to the bird, he would be a winged being: the bird knows nothing higher, nothing more blissful, than the winged condition. . . . Such as are a man's thoughts and dispositions, such is his God; so much worth as a man has, so much and no more has his God. Consciousness of God is self-consciousness, knowledge of God is self-knowledge. . . . There is no other essence which man can think, dream of, imagine, feel, believe in, wish for, love and adore as the *absolute,* than the essence of human nature itself.[3]

We are thus introduced to Feuerbach's interpretation of religion and of the objects with which religion deals. Let me first quote a few passages to present the theory in general terms, and then go on to some of the ways in which he works it out in detail.

The essence of religion is the immediate, involuntary, unconscious contemplation of the human nature as another, a distinct nature. . . . Religion is the relation of man to his own nature, . . . but to his nature not recognized as his own, but regarded as another nature, separate, nay contradistinguished from his own. . . . The contemplation of the human nature, a separately existent nature, is, however, in the original conception of religion an involuntary, childlike, simple act of the mind. . . . Religion is a dream, in which our own conceptions and emotions appear to us as separate existences, beings out of ourselves. The religious mind does not distinguish between subjective and objective—it has no doubts: it has the faculty not of discerning other things than itself, but of seeing its own conceptions out of itself as distinct beings.[4]

Feuerbach's undertaking, then, is to reduce "the supermundane, supernatural, and superhuman nature of God to the elements of human nature as its fundamental elements."[5] It will be sufficient for our purpose if we show how he deals with a group of problems which involve the conception of divine omnipotence. These are Prayer, Providence, and Creation.

Prayer is usually thought to be the confident appeal to the omnipotent will of God. But look closer, says Feuerbach. To pray is to be so absorbed in a passionate intensity of aspiration that all thought of the external world of man and nature is excluded. Prayer does not look for its objects to be attained by reliance on natural causes, nor is it aware of possible frustration. The deepest wishes of the heart are to succeed by their own unconditional affirmation. The man who prays is dominated by the

certainty that the power of the heart is greater than the power of Nature, that the heart's need is absolute necessity, the fate of the world. . . . The omnipotence to which man turns in prayer is nothing but the Omnipotence of Goodness, which, for the sake of the salvation of man, makes the impossible possible;—is, in truth nothing but the omnipotence of feeling which . . . wills that there be nothing else but feeling, nothing that contradicts the heart. . . . Omnipotence is the power before which no law, no external condition avails or subsists; but this power is the emotional nature, which feels every determination, every law, to be a limit, a restraint, and for that reason dismisses it. . . . In prayer man turns to the Omnipotence of Goodness;—which simply means, that in prayer man adores his own heart, regards his own feelings as absolute.[6]

"Belief in Providence is belief in a power to which all things stand at command to be used according to its pleasure, in opposition to which all the power of reality is nothing."[7] The proof of Providence is miracle. In miracle the operation of natural law is suspended or abolished: an event is brought about by the mere exercise of the divine will. But the acts we attribute to Providence are, says Feuerbach, acts performed exclusively for the sake of man. "We nowhere read that God, for the sake of brutes, became a brute, . . . or that God ever performed a miracle for the sake of animals or plants." Yet what is this but to assert the absolute efficacy of human ideals, the supreme power of human values?

Faith in Providence is faith in one's own worth, the faith of man in himself. . . . God concerns himself about me; he has in view my happiness, my salvation; he wills that I shall be blest, but that is my will also. . . . Thus God's love for me is nothing else than my self-love deified. When I believe in Providence, in what do I believe but in the divine reality and significance of my own being?[8]

In dealing with the problem of Creation you can say either that God created the world out of something or that he created it out of nothing. If he created it out of something, then he was limited by that something, as the artist by the medium he works in, and is not omnipotent. Religion, then, prefers to say he created it out of nothing. If we take that as a literal account of how the world came to be, then we have a mystery and not an explanation. Our experience contains no analogies to such a process. We may, however, read a different meaning into this doctrine of Creation. If the world was created by divine fiat, then there was a time when the world was not, and there may come a time when the world will pass away. On this showing, the world would have no necessary existence: it would depend on God's will: its ultimate power could be denied.

When thou sayest the world was made out of nothing, thou conceivest the world itself as nothing, thou clearest away from thy head all the limits to thy imagination, to thy feelings, to thy will. . . . In the inmost depths of thy soul thou wouldst rather there were no world, for where the world is there is matter, . . . limitation, and necessity. Nevertheless there *is* a world, there *is* matter. How dost thou escape from the dilemma of this contradiction? How dost thou expel the world from thy consciousness, that it may not disturb thee in the beatitude of thy unlimited soul? Only by making the world itself a product of will, by giving it an arbitrary existence always hovering between existence and nonexistence, always awaiting its annihilation.[9]

Once again we reach the position that divine omnipotence is simply the omnipotence of the human will. Following the same line of thought Feuerbach concludes that the God of religion is nothing but human nature objectified and deified.

He attempts to reinforce this conclusion by showing that the persistent problems about God's nature arise from a failure to perceive the identity of the divine with the human. If the supernatural is intractable to reason, as we maintained in our first chapter, that is because theology and philosophy have attributed to God a distinct and separate existence from man.[10]

If it seems absurd to suggest that religion can dispense with the belief in an independent god, Feuerbach asks us to examine what we mean by independence. The term, he thinks, necessarily carries with it the idea of separate existence in space and time. "Real, sensational existence is that which is not dependent on my own mental spontaneity or activity, but by which I am involuntarily affected, which is when I am not, when I do not think of it or feel it. The existence of God must therefore be in space. . . ."[11] Theology may choose between two ways of meeting this problem. It may say that God exists spiritually. This means that he is not perceived by the senses, but is to be spiritually discerned. But spiritual discernment is not a universal endowment, and it is intermittent in operation. To assign to God a spiritual existence is merely an ambiguous way of saying that he exists only in the feelings and aspirations of the human mind. On the other hand, theology may attribute to God

a sensational existence, to which however all the conditions of sensational existence are wanting:—consequently an existence at once sensational and not sensational, an existence which contradicts the idea of the sensational, or only a vague existence in general, which is fundamentally a sensational one, but which, in order that this may not become evident, is divested of all the predicates of a real sensational existence. But such an "existence in general" is self-contradictory.[12]

Most of us, I think, must have felt the sting of the problem which Feuerbach is attacking. On the one hand, a god who is a merely spiritual being is not wholly convincing: he lacks that quality of literalness, known to us in sense experience, which seems necessary to reality in its full meaning. It would be much easier to believe in a god who heard or spoke or saw, and skepticism would be rarer if the heavens were not always silent. There are times when we crave an idol to worship. Yet an idol, after all, is only an idol. A god with a body, who existed in space and time, would be subject to all the limitations of finitude, and would satisfy as little as the purely spiritual being. Thus we are caught upon the horns of a dilemma. God must be such that his existence can be empirically verified, yet, paradoxically, such a god, if we found him, would not be the God we seek. Feuerbach's escape from the dilemma is perhaps too facile. Dismiss the idea of the transcendent deity, he says, as illusory; realize that God is wholly immanent, and your problem will disappear. You will cease to talk of man's relation to an independent divinity: you will be content to recognize the divinity of man.

We need not follow Feuerbach in his elaboration of

the contradictions in religious thought. He gives an extraordinarily searching account of these traditional perplexities, but we have gone far enough to perceive the general outlines of his interpretation of religion. His answer to our original question now becomes clear. Religion conveys no insight into an invisible supernatural reality, for there is no such reality. What we may learn from it is not truth about God, but truth about man. In religion the feelings, the secret desires and aspirations, the latent energies of men, are exposed to view. God, Creation, Miracle, Salvation, Immortality, are imaginative projections of human longings and human self-confidence. Religion is a kind of earnest poetry. Its metaphors and symbols are not to be taken literally. So to take them is the error of theology. A sound philosophy will avoid this mistake and will disengage the element of truth in religious doctrine from the symbolical form in which it is presented.

Our first thought, I suppose, as we survey this theory, is that religion will repudiate any such account of its meaning. For it is thus reduced to illusion—beneficent illusion in many respects, if you like, but still illusion. We thought we were worshiping God; it turns out that we were really worshiping man. We thought that we had found a way out into the divine; it seems that we had only been exploring the depths of the soul. It is idle for Feuerbach to repeat that religion is naïve and does not make the distinction between symbol and thing symbolized which later reflection imposes. Now that Feuerbach has written his work and exposed the illusion, religion cannot return to the stage of intellectual innocence. His, in short, is one of those unfortunate theories which are in danger of being falsified as soon as they become public property. The Hedonist doctrine that pleasure is the only object of desire is an example of what I mean. Hedonism may have been true as an account of human motive until it was formulated, but, after that, anyone who is told that the law of his being is to seek pleasure may falsify the law and assert his freedom by choosing something other than pleasure as his goal. The chief value of Hedonism is that it gives us an opportunity to avoid being pleasure seekers. Schopenhauer's doctrine that men are the deluded victims of a blind Cosmic Will is another example. Schopenhauer, at least, has seen through Nature's trickery and need no longer be deceived. And in letting the cat out of the bag he has enlightened the rest of us. We can now take steps to free ourselves from the tyranny of this monstrous Will. And so with Feuerbach. After reading him, we shall not again surrender to the illusion of religion. Yet that surely is an unsatisfactory explanation of religion which explains religion away, an unimpressive science which ends by annihilating its own subject matter.

If this objection seems unconvincing because it does not deal with Feuerbach's analysis on its own merits, let us essay a slightly different line of attack. His account of religion suffers from the fact that it is the account of one who is observing, not of one who is experiencing. If instead of trying to report what it *looks* like to be religious, we try to report what it *feels* like, we shall find confirmation of our original assertion that religion cannot dispense with the claim to be in touch with a divine reality other than man. Let me briefly illustrate what I mean. Prayer, says Feuerbach, is the unrestrained expression of human desire, the articulate utterance of the deepest longings of a soul forgetful of anything that might impede or frustrate them. Prayer, that is, is purely exclamatory. This seems to me to omit what is essential. For I can distinguish between a sigh, let us say, and a prayer, and the difference is this, that prayer, whether as worship or petition, expects to be heard. It is directed to another intelligence. Cancel that external reference and what you have left is not prayer. It is mere lyricism seeking and finding automatically its own relief.

Again, religion inspires loyalty, devotion, love toward the ideal. I do not see how one can entertain these sentiments toward an abstract ideal—which is all that Feuerbach will grant. I can make nothing of the notion of the expression of loyalty or love for its own sake. That is mere animal behavior. The essence of loyalty and love is the conviction that their tributes are accepted and valued by another being.

Finally, consider Feuerbach's statement that faith in divine omnipotence is nothing but faith in the power of man. Surely that misses completely the quality of religious optimism; for that power with which religion claims to be able to overcome the world is derivative, not original; its confidence and its victory are vicarious, made possible by reliance on a Supreme Power whose strength is made perfect in man's weakness. If Feuerbach were right, religion would be no more than a sublime and ridiculous attempt to sustain our courage by raising our voice.

The force of this criticism is perhaps concealed from Feuerbach by his use of certain conveniently ambiguous terms. I refer to expressions like, The divine nature is the human nature *externalized, projected, taken objectively*. They are ambiguous because they do not make clear whether the operation referred to is supposed to be done consciously or unconsciously; they are convenient because you can choose the meaning which suits the context of the moment. In any event, we are asked to believe that what takes place in religion is this: certain states of mind, such as joy, peace, confidence, ecstasy, by virtue of their quality and effects, come to be called divine. "Feeling is pronounced to be religious simply because it is feeling. . . . But is not feeling thereby declared to be itself the absolute, the divine? If feeling in itself is good, religious, i.e. holy, divine, has not feeling its God in itself?"[13] The state of mind is then referred to a divine being as its object of cause. It is externalized and deified. Whether the process is conscious or unconscious need not here concern us. Our difficulty turns on the conception of a *mere* state of mind, that is, of a mental event which in the first instance has no reference to anything beyond itself. Frankly, there is no such thing. Surely we have listened to the teaching of philosophical idealism to little purpose if we have not learned that the mind is not a thing, but rather a way of referring to or dealing with things. Every state of mind points beyond itself:

an idea is an idea *of* something, an attitude is an attitude *toward* something, a feeling is a feeling *about* something. A simple illustration may help to make this clear. Suppose you want to feel cheerful, how do you go about it? Surely not by trying to induce that feeling by any of the now popular methods of autosuggestion. Those will not bring you the real thing. If you recover cheerfulness through drink or drugs or companionship or books, that is because these things open up to you features of the world which you had ignored or forgotten. You regain cheerfulness by discovering something to be cheerful about. And there is no other way. If it should turn out that there is nothing whatever in life to be cheerful about, then cheerfulness will be ever beyond us. Apply this to the feelings called religious; to the states of mind which Feuerbach says we label divine. It then becomes clear that there can be no religious feeling unless there is something to feel religious about: if there is a God then certain feeling may be called divine—not otherwise. Thus I believe that Feuerbach has exactly reversed the true order. He says we begin with feeling, find it divine, and call in God to explain it. I hold that we begin with the experience of God and then find the experience divine.

A little while ago I said that the religious man would naturally repudiate any suggestion that his belief rested on mistaking the human for the divine. No one likes to be told that his most cherished convictions are illusory. Yet there is something more at stake here than offended vanity, and I wish to consider some of the consequences that follow from confronting religion with Feuerbach's interpretation of its meaning. His position is essentially the same as that of Positivism. Religion is the childhood of the human mind. The child lives in a world of imagination; so does religion. The child thinks that all its desires will be gratified; so does religion. In matters of belief and conduct the child is dependent on external aid and support; so is religion. Growth in maturity means learning to distinguish between pictures and realities, between fancies and facts; it means also learning the difficult art of self-reliance. It is this enlightenment of maturity which systems like those of Feuerbach offer to religion. Guided by philosophy, religion is to discover its true nature. My question is, What becomes of religion in the process?

The only possible answer would seem to be this: that religion dies of disillusionment. Every advance in science, in philosophy, in general culture, means so much ground lost for religion. A progressively vanishing factor in human affairs, its destiny is that it shall be superseded by a condition of life in which man, assured of self-knowledge and relying on his own powers, will move confidently in a world that has been cleared of illusion. If it survive, it will be only as a wistful memory of lost innocence and lost joys; its function will be that of a dream which invests the sober landscape of experience with an ancient glamor and to whose influence we shall surrender only in hours of. forgetfulness or fatigue.

Yet it is conceivable that we might continue to think

of religion as the stage of childhood in the life of the mind and still assign to it something more than a temporary value. Feuerbach, I think, is hardly willing to admit that it will ever wholly outlive its usefulness, and certainly those writers today whose thought has a close affinity with his dwell insistently on the moral and spiritual values of religion even after its metaphysical pretensions have been exposed. Christianity has made us familiar with the idea of the likeness between religion and the mind of the child. Candor and simplicity are characteristic of the child s manner of regard, and these are counted as virtues, for if his world lacks complexity it also lacks the confusion of the more developed outlook. Religion too is naïve: its vision is relatively untroubled and its speech unrhetorical. This is as it should be. When man faces the ultimate in any form—be it danger or death or some moving revelation of truth or beauty—he is forced back on simple thought and simple language. And in the presence of God learning and nice discrimination and an elegant style are out of place. Now to become as a little child in this sense is generally held to be an injunction that it is both possible and desirable to carry out. The contemplation of nature, the enjoyment of art, the cultivation of mystical religion all make for a certain childlike simplification of vision, and they are all regarded as recurrent needs in the economy of the good life. The question that here concerns us is, How, in the case of religion, can one justify this retreat into immaturity, this apparent surrender of reason? Now if religion is the thing that Feuerbach says it is—a region of illusion and dream—then justification is impossible. Once we have outgrown dream and toys it is as discreditable to go back to them as it is to seek solace in drugs. If through enlightenment we have outgrown religion, then we should put it behind us for good.

Feuerbach says that the distinction between the child and the adult is this: the former sees figuratively what the latter sees literally. Let us draw the distinction in a different way. Let us say that the child sees something that the adult forgets or covers up with his accumulated knowledge. Then the attempt to recapture the child's vision would not be a cult of dreams for dreams' sake; it would be the search to recover truth which only the child's insight reveals. From this point of view, you could justify religion as a permanent and not merely a vanishing factor in human life. But you would then be regarding it as a source of genuine insight not otherwise attainable: it would be more than the vision of immaturity: it would have its own unique view of the world. But this function is just what Feuerbach denies to religion.

His theory then has to confront these alternatives: either you say that the destiny of religion is to pass away as human enlightenment advances—in which event we should talk not of the future of religion but of "the irreligion of the future"; or you say that religion is to remain with us as a perpetual source of moral and spiritual inspiration—and then you are forced to admit that religion possesses knowledge peculiar to itself.

This brief account of Feuerbach's teaching may serve to exhibit a fairly typical expression of the symbolical theory of religious knowledge. I say typical, because although Feuerbach is often inadequate or obscure,—particularly in his concept of Humanity,—yet he permits us to see both the characteristic design and the characteristic strength and weakness of the theory. Moreover, one cannot fail to notice how modern are many of the ideas which dominate his work. His humanism, his emphasis on divine immanence, his subjectivism, his conception of religion as allied to poetry rather than to science or philosophy, his contention that religion is preoccupied with value and not with existence—all these represent tendencies which powerfully affect our thinking today. In the next chapter I shall study how some of these themes introduced by Feuerbach have been developed by later reflection.

CHAPTER IV

SYMBOLICAL THEORIES: SABATIER, SANTAYANA

THE preceding chapter was devoted to a study of Feuerbach. Basing our account on his work, *The Meaning of Christianity*, we distinguished and criticized his fundamental ideas upon the general nature and truth of religion. We promised to show in the present chapter how some of these ideas have been developed in the course of later reflection. Feuerbach's conclusion, let me recall, is that the function of religion is not to convey knowledge about superhuman realities, but to reveal the depths of human nature. Religion objectifies human attributes and calls them divine. In religion man unconsciously adores his own latent nature.

There are many, and I confess that I am of their number, who find it hard to be patient when faced with this kind of doctrine. One does not need to be pessimist or cynic to feel that man is one of the poorest substitutes for God that ingenuity can propose. It is better to repudiate religion and all its works than to chatter about worshiping or adoring humanity. If we are told that what is meant is not mankind as it actually is, but mankind in its ideal aspect, even then our outraged sense of fitness is hardly pacified: there still seems something insufferably provincial, nay presumptuous, in the thought of identifying the hu-

man and the divine. Yet it will not do to surrender
uncritically to these wholly natural reflections. We are
dealing with a type of theory that has commended itself
to men whose regard for religion, whose modesty,
sincerity, and intellectual grasp cannot be called in
question. It becomes our business, therefore, to discover
if we can what are the motives and reasons that have
led to conclusions which to their authors at any rate
have seemed convincing.

Every significant assertion implies a negation. When
the assertion, taken by itself, is hard to understand,
its meaning often becomes clear from an examination
of the corresponding negation. The positive statement
in the situation before us is, to put it crudely: God is
another name for Man. Let us ask what is the negation
behind this and see if we gain any light. What, then,
does a representative of the symbolical theory deny?
Let me put words into his mouth.

If by the statement, "God exists," you mean that in addition to all finite selves there is a being called God, numerically
distinct from them, an independent centre of consciousness,
with his own unique life and purposes, with a differential
activity of his own, then it is not true that this being exists.

Our question then is: How is this conclusion reached?
In trying to frame an answer it will be well to have
some particular author in mind, and so the account
I am about to give will be based largely on Sabatier's
well-known work, *Esquisse d'une philosophie de la religion*. Although I shall not often quote from him di-

rectly, what I say will be found to have support in his text.

The general problem which Sabatier, and for that matter every other student of the philosophy of religion, has to face is this: how to reconcile the apparently conflicting elements which religion finds or postulates in God. On the one hand He is the ideal being, the sum of perfection: He is perfect love, goodness, wisdom, justice. In Him the restless heart finds rest. On the other hand, He is the Supreme Being, the most powerful, the most real, the Creator and Sustainer upon whom the destiny of man and nature ultimately depends. How can he be both? For example, if God is the creator of everything, then He is responsible for evil, but how can perfect goodness be the author of evil? Here is the source of those interminable disputes which have vexed the theologian and the philosopher. If God as Supreme Value cannot be harmonized with God as Supreme Existent then one of the claims must go. The theory we are now to follow rejects the contention that God is the Supreme Existent.

The first line of thought whose influence we may here trace goes back to Kant. In his analysis of organized knowledge Kant distinguishes between the form of knowledge, which is supplied by the mind, and the material of knowledge, which is supplied by experience—ultimately by sense experience. Either of these factors is infertile without the other. Thus the necessary forms of thought cannot operate in a void: they are unproductive—there is no cognition of real objects without the material furnished by the crude data of sense. The world of valid experience, the so-called phenomenal world, everywhere exhibits the interplay of these two factors. It follows that we cannot be said, strictly speaking, to know any object that is wholly devoid of sensuous content: it cannot appear within the world of our experience. Now God is, admittedly, a being that does not report itself to sense. God, therefore, cannot be rationally known: there can be no science of God. Now we do not need to adopt Kant's epistemology to see that he is stating a truth as important as it is perhaps obvious. God is not to be found as a natural object: he has no body: he is not seen or heard or touched: if he works in or upon nature, his work is impossible to detect. Moreover, we do not *expect* to find him in nature either as a prodigious being or in some as yet undiscovered recesses where he operates as the greatest of the natural forces. We should not dream of trying to verify his existence as we should that of some problematic entity, say the sea serpent or the leprechaun. And as little should we think of finding him as one person among others. We may say that we believe that God exists, but that does not mean that we should consider verifying his existence as we should that of some person, say Mrs. Harris, whose existence was open to doubt. The idea of sending out a theological expedition to prove or disprove the existence of God may seem irreverent, but in the first instance it is absurd.

Nevertheless, it may be said, the expression "God

exists" must have a legitimate meaning, because have
we not got the traditional proofs of the existence of
God? Sabatier would reply that, quite apart from any
question about their logical validity, the being whose
existence they establish is not entitled to be called divine. Consider just one of the so-called proofs, that
which is based on the necessity for a First Cause, and
the meaning of this will become clear. For the moment,
the particular form given to the argument is a matter
of indifference: the essence of it in any form is this:
Nature is not self-explanatory; we must therefore postulate some uncaused Cause upon which it depends. Nature is the effect; we infer a cause; we call this Cause
God. It is the last step which must be called in question.
We ought not to designate any being divine who is not
holy, wise, and good. But there is nothing in the argument that justifies us in investing the First Cause with
these attributes. There need be no more in the cause
than in the effect. Nature has not been shown to be holy
or wise or good. Unless we surreptitiously endow the
First Cause with moral attributes its existence is, in
Lecky's striking expression, "a mere question of archae-
ology."[1] The criticism is, of course, familiar. Its interest for us is that it shows that an object whose existence
could be demonstrated by science or philosophy will not
suffice as a religious object, for it is incapable of excit-
ing the religious interest. There is nothing in the idea
of the first cause to evoke reverence or worship. As
one of the characters in a recent novel remarks, "God
as a sense of warmth about the heart, God as exulta-

tion, God as tears in the eyes, God as a rush of power or thought—that was all right. But God as truth, God as $2 + 2 = 4$—that wasn't so clearly all right."[2] Philosophy must always face this predicament with regard to religion, for philosophy will find God, if at all, as a "He Who" or a "That Which" is responsible for the universe, with an explanation of the universe —and religion is not primarily interested in explanations. The God of religion is not a God who *explains* the world, but a God who is superior to it and hence overcomes it. The God who is mere Fact will not engender religion and is therefore not God. The history of religion is there to confirm it. Religions do not have their origin in scientific fact or philosophic truth however profound, but in inspired personalities who awaken passion and communicate enthusiasm; only under the influence of the feelings and sentiments thus aroused does the world of fact and external objects become spiritually significant. Thus, so the argument runs, God must first be found within before he can be found without. It is this interior God who is known in the heart and conscience of man that is the real God of religion.

This is brought out clearly if we look for a moment at another item of religious doctrine—the belief in miracle. A miracle is an event that reveals God in operation. But what is the criterion by which this event is distinguished as divine? At first sight we may reply, "The fact that it contradicts the ordinary course of nature." A moment's reflection shows us that we are in error. Mere irregularity is not enough to constitute miracle; if so, anything that was fortuitous or inexplicable would be miraculous. The event must manifest significant purpose. As one writer puts it:

What surprises us in the miracle is that, contrary to what is usually the case, we can see a real and just ground for it. Thus, if the water of Lourdes, bottled and sold by chemists, cured all diseases, there would be no miracle, but only a new scientific discovery. In such a case, we should no more know why we were cured than we now know why we were created. But if each believer in taking the water thinks the effect morally conditioned, if he interprets the result, should it be favourable, as an answer to his faith and prayers, then the cure becomes miraculous because it becomes intelligible and manifests the obedience of nature to the exigencies of spirit.[3]

In other words, miracle is one of those rare occasions when an event happens because it *ought* to and not because it must, and so confirms our faith in some universal fitness or justice in things. But we must first have this faith in a divine teleological order, independently arrived at, before we can designate any event miraculous. It is the spiritual construction that the mind puts on the event and not the event by itself which is religiously significant. From this point of view Sabatier contends that it is possible to accept the scientist's rejection of miracle and still preserve all that is essential to faith. Science, he says, cannot unify the causal series in a closed system: that is, it cannot make general statements about the totality of things; it is confined to the study of secondary causes. But faith, or piety as he calls it, may regard the world in its entirety as dependent upon God. "Les lois de la nature, qui nous sont apparues, depuis lors, dans leur constance souveraine, deviennent immédiatement, pour la piété, l'expression de la volonté de Dieu."[4] Thus, since every event ultimately flows from the divine will, any event may to the eye of spiritual discernment be regarded as a miracle, as a revelation of God. God is not in the event, but in the discernment.[5]

I referred a few moments ago to the influence of Kant. Our account would be incomplete without a reference to another great figure in the history of thought—Pascal. Pascal pictures man as set down between two incomprehensibles, the infinitely great at one end of the scale, the infinitely small at the other. But man's condition is not hopeless, because he is aware of it. "L'homme n'est qu'un roseau, le plus faible de la nature; mais c'est un roseau pensant. . . . Toute notre dignité consiste donc en la pensée."[6] He differs from the brute in that he is capable of self-criticism: he can carry this even to the point of hating himself. In thus recognizing his imperfections he exhibits the working in him of an ideal of perfection, the source not only of his greatest misery, but of his highest joy. Of joy, because "thou wouldst not be seeking me hadst thou not already found me," and thus the very seeking is itself a sort of finding. And where should we seek God but in aspiration and longing and ecstasy? "C'est le coeur qui sent Dieu et non la raison. Voilà ce que c'est que la foi: Dieu sensible au coeur, non à la raison."[7] "Nous ne pouvons aimer ce qui est hors de nous, il faut aimer un être qui soit en nous. . . . Le royaume de

Dieu est en nous, le bien universel est en nous, est nous-même. . . ."[8]*

With a writer like Pascal it is always hard to know how much one may legitimately read into his statements, but I do not think we are doing violence to his thought if we attribute to him a fairly definite doctrine of human nature which we may express somewhat as follows. Man is incomplete; he is still in the making. Therefore you cannot say what he really is unless you take into account what he will be, or better, what he wills to be. He is a subject and not an object, and therefore his ideals are the most important part of him. They are literally a part of him, for an ideal which is actively willed is more than a mere ideal: it is actual. Indeed, we might say, if we care for this kind of expression, that will is the point where ideality and actuality coincide. Thus we take the will for the deed, we give credit for good intentions, we say that repentance is the beginning of holiness, for to repent the evil deed is to disown it, and to disown it is the beginning of freedom from it. "Thou couldst not seek holiness hadst thou not already found it." The divine unrest

* I am far from wishing to imply that Pascal was committed to a doctrine of God as wholly immanent. In the passage quoted above I have deliberately omitted words of crucial importance. Pascal says, "Un être qui soit en nous, *et qui ne soit pas nous.* . . ." "Le bien universel est nous-même, *et n'est pas nous.*" Cf. also "Toute religion est fausse, qui, dans sa foi, n'adore pas un Dieu comme principe de toutes choses, et qui, dans sa morale, n'aime pas un seul Dieu comme objet de toutes choses. Mais il est impossible que Dieu soit jamais la fin, s'il n'est le principe."[9] "Incompréhensible que Dieu soit, et incompréhensible qu'il ne soit pas. . . ."[10] The extraordinary force of Pascal is in large part due to the vigor with which he maintains both the immanence and the transcendence of God; but at the moment it was his emphasis on the former that I was concerned to make clear.

of the human spirit is thus really divine, for it bears witness to man's grasp on that which is beyond him.

Here, then, we seem to have a way of answering the question, What does "the presence of God" really mean? We have seen that it does not mean the empirical apparition to sense of some external being; it can only mean his presence in feeling and desire. The name generally given to that experience in which man suffers the visitation of God is inspiration. But, as Sabatier puts it, there are no external remarks of inspiration— as though a being from without had touched the soul. The inspiration of the prophet does not make him abnormal; on the contrary, it is a heightening of normal human powers. The prophet differs from other men in greater clearness and range of ideas, in an intenser conviction, in a more vehement passion, in a gift of poetry and eloquence. He does not lose his personality: he finds it exalted. "L'inspiration religieuse n'est pas autre chose que la pénétration organique de l'homme par Dieu; mais, nous le répétons encore, par un Dieu tout intérieur. . . ."[11] Thus once again we have reason to assert the existence of the God that is within, to deny the existence of the God that is without.

Reviewing the evidence, I think we are forced to admit that an impressive case has been established for this conclusion. Whatever questions or feelings of compunction we may have about the idea of a God that is within, we cannot overlook the difficulties in the idea of transcendence. As against all deistic tendencies, as against any theory that makes much of the separateness of man and God, Sabatier is true, I believe, both to logic and to religion. Moreover, it is worth while to have had it made clear that religion is not in the first instance founded on the perception of fact nor on philosophical or scientific truths alone. Religion is not to be confused either with history or science or philosophy; and to see this is to be on the way to discovering whatever is unique in religion. All this is clear gain.

It is when we examine the doctrine on its positive side that our difficulties begin. Grant that we can make little or nothing of the literal external God, what does it mean to speak of a God who is wholly within? Sabatier writes:

Mais l'objet de la connaissance religieuse ou morale, Dieu, le Bien, le Beau, ce ne sont pas là des phénomènes, qu'on puisse saisir hors du moi et indépendamment de lui. Dieu ne se révèle que dans et par la piété; le Bien que dans la conscience de l'homme, le Beau que dans l'activité créatrice de l'artiste.[12]

That seems to me equivalent to saying that God exists only when and as he is felt. We do not introduce ambiguity and complexity into our ethical or aesthetic theories by externalizing and personifying the Good or the Beautiful; what justification have we for doing so when it comes to religion? The passage I have quoted seems clearly to mean that God is simply another name for man praying, or worshiping, or experiencing any emotion that you choose to call religious. In that event it would be better to drop the name God from our vocabulary. But Sabatier is not willing to

go to that extreme. In several passages he shows that
he is aware of the objection. Here is one of them. "On
objecte que la piété humaine et l'éveil du sentiment
religieux doivent avoir une cause objective, et cette
cause ne saurait être que la révélation même de Dieu.
Rien n'est plus juste. . . ."[13] But of course he could
not without fatal consequences to his theory elaborate
this conception of an independent deity who is the
cause of religious feeling. And on the whole I think
we must see in him another exponent of humanism,
another disciple of unqualified immanence. This finds
confirmation in his treatment of religious knowledge.
One of the essential characters of that knowledge is
that it is symbolic. It depicts the eternal by means of
the temporal, the spiritual through the sensible, the
invisible by the visible. All theology is figurative. But
its mysteries are the mysteries of the human soul; its
truths are truths of human experience; its insight is
insight into the feelings.[14]

What seems to me the fundamental error in Sabatier's position is the error common to all symbolical
theories of religion. They point out, and quite rightly,
that religion does not and cannot take its rise in the
perception of fact or of bare truth. You cannot by evidence or demonstration argue a person into religion
any more than you can argue him into falling in love.
But it does not follow, as those I am criticizing seem
to think it follows, that religion can dispense with
fact and literal truth altogether. The historical facts
of the Crucifixion and the Resurrection will not of
themselves suffice to induce a conviction of salvation.

If you say that therefore the historical facts themselves are irrelevant, that the truths they symbolize are alone important, that we can hold to the truths and let history go, then you simply confuse religion with philosophy. For when you have the truths without the historical symbols what you have is philosophy and not religion. Religion cannot take its rise from historical fact, but it cannot sustain its life without it. In the same way, religions, it is true, are not founded by philosophers propounding a system, but by prophets or other inspired persons who are dominated by emotion and not by reason, and whose utterances are colored by passion rather than by logic. Yet the appeal of the prophet is never merely to feeling: he is no rhetorician depending on some display of personal excitement. His force and his authority come from his conviction that he has a message to deliver or a revelation to communicate. Apart from that conviction he would simply be exploiting his own emotional eccentricities, and his legacy would not be disciples or a church but the transient excitement of a mob. But the claim to revelation is a claim to insight, to truth.

Up to this point we have confined our attention to the negative side of the symbolical theory. I wish now, with Santayana as guide, to take a glance at its positive teaching. If religion is not to be taken as literal truth, how is it to be taken? The answer usually given is, "As a kind of poetry." I am not sure whether this is a polite way of dismissing it as illusion, or whether it implies something less uncomplimentary. The symbolists themselves have left us in doubt—with one exception. In several of his essays, and in his book *Reason in Religion,* Mr. Santayana has given to this theme the most intelligent and the most distinguished treatment that, so far as I know, it has received. Let us see what he has to tell us.

I should make it clear at the outset that I am not attributing to Santayana in any wholesale manner the ideas that we have found in Feuerbach or Sabatier. But there is a general affinity between his position and theirs which justifies us in treating them together. That affinity comes out clearly enough in passages such as the following. "The idea that religion contains a literal, not a symbolic, representation of truth and life is simply an impossible idea. Whoever entertains it has not come within the region of profitable philosophizing on that subject."[15] "The insoluble problems [of theology] . . . are artificial problems, unknown to philosophy before it betook itself to the literal justification of fables in which the objects of rational endeavour were represented as causes of natural existence."[16]

The inference is that if we are to avoid these fearful errors and contradictions we must interpret religion differently. Religion and poetry, then, are identical in essence in that they both express operations of the imagination. What is imagination? The mind's ambition exceeds its powers. Man desires truth, a coherent picture of reality; he desires social and political harmony; he desires moral order and perfection; he aspires, in short, after a world in which, as a rational being, he can find himself at home. The senses and the understanding, the instruments with which he has to work, are inadequate for this task. Here the imagination comes to the rescue: it tries prophetically to satisfy human ambition by anticipating and correcting the understanding. Wholly free and disinterested in its operation, it emancipates us from the deadening influence of routine and from that narrow view of things which the requirements of practical life continually impose on us. By vividly presenting the ideal it stimulates us to pursue it. "It gives us refreshment and a foretaste of that perfect adaptation of things to our faculties and of our faculties to things which, could it extend to every part of experience, would constitute the ideal life."[17] Poetry thus improves life by imagining it improved; by giving us another world to live in, it helps us to remold that world which we have nearer to the heart's desire.

The function of religion is the same. Its purpose is to transform the actual by showing it transfigured in the light of the ideal. By clarifying and invigorating human ambition it sets that ambition over against circumstance with power to transform it. It holds up, for example,

the ideal of deity, which is nothing but the ideal of man freed from those limitations which a humble and wise man accepts for himself, but which a spiritual man never ceases to feel as limitations. Man, for instance, is mortal, and his whole animal and social economy is built on that fact, so that his practical ideal must start on that basis, and make the best of it; but immortality is essentially better, and the eternal is in many ways constantly present to a noble mind; the gods therefore are immortal, and to speak their language in prayer is to learn to see all things as they do, and as reason must, under the form of eternity.[18]

Let me follow Mr. Santayana in his treatment of prayer, hinted at in the last quotation. Nothing more eloquent or more moving has, I believe, been written on the subject, and a study of this particular instance will give us the clue to his whole interpretation.

In rational prayer the soul may be said to accomplish three things important to its welfare: it withdraws within itself and defines its good, it accommodates itself to destiny, and it grows like the ideal it conceives. . . .

Prayer, in fine, though it accomplishes nothing material, constitutes something spiritual. It will not bring rain, but until rain comes it may cultivate hope and resignation and may prepare the heart for any issue, opening up a vista in which human prosperity will appear in its conditioned existence and conditional value. A candle wasting itself before an image will prevent no misfortune, but it may bear witness to some silent hope or relieve some sorrow by expressing it; it may soften a little the bitter sense of impotence which would consume a mind aware of physical dependence but not of spiritual dominion. Worship, supplication, reliance on the gods, express both these things in an appropriate parable. Physical impotence is expressed by man's appeal for help; moral dominion by belief in God's omnipotence. This belief may afterwards seem to be contradicted by events. It would be so in truth if God's omnipotence stood for a material magical control of events by the values they were to generate. But the believer knows in his heart, in spite of the confused explanations he may give of his feelings, that a material efficacy is not the test of his faith. His faith will survive any outward disappointment. In fact, it will grow by that discipline and not become truly religious until it ceases to be a foolish expectation of improbable things and rises on stepping-stones of its material disappointments into a spiritual peace. What would sacrifice be but a risky investment if it did not redeem us from the love of those things which it asks us to surrender? What would be the miserable fruit of an appeal to God which, after bringing us face to face with him, left us still immersed in what we could have enjoyed without him? The real use and excuse for magic is this, that by enticing us, in the service of natural lusts, into a region above natural instrumentalities, it accustoms us to that rarer atmosphere, so that we may learn to breathe it for its own sake. By the time we discover the mechanical futility of religion we may have begun to blush at the thought of using religion mechanically; for what should be the end of life if friendship with the gods is a means only? When thaumaturgy is discredited, the childish desire to work miracles may itself have passed away. Before we weary of the attempt to hide and piece out our mortality, our concomitant immortality may have dawned upon us. While we are waiting for the command to take up our bed and walk we may hear a voice saying: Thy sins are forgiven thee.

This passage makes clear, I think, what Santayana means by saying that religion transforms life by idealizing it. Yet this advantage, he goes on to say, is neutralized, and this function distorted, by an abuse to which religion is subject. By some strange fatality, which he does not explain, religion insists on taking its fancies for facts. Not content with presenting us with an ideal picture, it tries to persuade mankind that "in spite of appearances, the world is really such as that rather arbitrary idealisation has painted it."

Its myths and parables are offered as substitutes for history and science. The Creation and the Fall are deprived at once of their symbolic significance and their moral virtue by being regarded as events that literally took place. The doctrines of Heaven and Hell instead of reflecting figuratively, as they should, the truth that moral choices are of critical importance, pretend to be information about transmundane reality. On this showing religion suffers from an excess of imagination and is hardly to be distinguished from superstition. Indeed, Santayana does not hesitate to make the identification. Religion and superstition are, he says, the same in origin; that is, in both, the fancy attaches its images to facts and things instead of to ideals.[19] How then, we may ask, has religion managed to survive?—for in the long run nothing founded on error and superstition can hold its own. Santayana replies that religion is a luckily beneficent superstition; its fancies have had the good fortune to be morally significant. This, as he is careful to point out, does not mean that they are true in any literal or demonstrable sense. The intuitions of faith are called true "not because their necessary correspondence to truth can be demonstrated, but because a man dwelling on these intuitions is conscious of a certain moral transformation, of a certain warmth and energy of life."[20] From this point of view it is perfectly consistent for him to write:

Religions will thus be better or worse, never true or false. . . . Matters of religion should never be matters of controversy. We neither argue with a lover about his taste, nor condemn him, if we are just, for knowing so human a passion. . . . But while we acquiesce in his experience and are glad he has it, we need no arguments to dissuade us from sharing it. Each man may have his own loves, but the object in each case is different. And so it is, or should be, in religion. . . . To the religious man religion is inwardly justified. God has no need of natural or logical witnesses, but speaks himself within the heart.[21]

This, then, is what it means to call religion poetry. Like love and like poetry it is its own justification. To deny the pretensions of religion to literal validity should as little disturb religion as it disturbs the "artist's pleasure to be warned that the beauty he expresses has no objective existence."[22]

My first comment on this conclusion is that I do not find the comparison illuminating. Religion, we are told, is a kind of poetry, and poetry is mere poetry ("Art for Art's sake")—but what is *mere* poetry? Of course, it is obvious that the metaphors of the poet are metaphors and not literal statements, that the painting is not a photograph, and that the novel and the drama do not describe real persons or events that really happened. But I do not think we can go on from this to say that art is nothing but the play of the imagination, that it lives in a world of its own, and that it has no connection with truth or reality. I realize that I am here treading on difficult and controversial ground, and I have no time to do justice to the argument. I can only state my own convictions dogmatically. If I take a broad vision of the function of art I find myself forced to say that it is in some sense, very difficult to define, a source of insight. The drama and the novel, though they are fictions, yet tell me truth about human nature; the poem reveals elements of beauty and order in experience; and music conveys the sense of levels of reality concealed from ordinary perception. All significant art, I should say, is ultimately a form of revelation, and you simply impoverish its meaning if you reduce it to the mere exercise of the imagination, however delightful and tonic that may be. If this is so, nothing is gained by saying that religion is poetry, for both claim to confer insight and with neither of them can you reduce the insight to the form of rational propositions.

Let me turn from these general considerations to a specific criticism. Santayana has dwelt upon the moral and spiritual value of religion. He has further told us that "what successful religion should really pass into is contemplation, ideality, poetry."[23] The question I ask is, Will religion continue to promote these values when this consummation has taken place? If we take religion as poetry will it continue to nourish our minds as it did when we took it literally? The answer is that it will not. For recall Santayana's account of prayer. "Prayer, though it accomplishes nothing material, constitutes something spiritual. It will not bring rain, but until rain comes it may cultivate hope and resignation and may prepare the heart for any issue. . . ." It is clear from this that if one is to gain these spiritual benefits one must pray not for these benefits, but for rain. The very condition for getting them is that you should be superstitious and unenlightened. It will not do for you to have read Santayana. Further, if your prayer is, in Santayana's words, merely "a soliloquy expressing need," and not a petition addressed to a power who is believed to hear it, then either you will cease to pray or you will not experience its spiritual efficacy.

If this criticism seems too familiar, I will say only two things in reply. First, that it is not more common than the error against which it is directed, and, secondly, that I must continue to wonder at the capacity for self-deception among sophisticated minds. My feelings in this matter have been perfectly expressed by Mr. Walter Lippmann when he writes:

When the truths of religion have lost their connection with a superhuman order, the cord of their life is cut. What remains is a somewhat archaic, a somewhat questionable, although a very touching, quaint medley of poetry, rhetoric, fable, exhortation, and insight into human travail. When Mr. Santayana says that "matters of religion should never be matters of controversy" because "we never argue with a lover about his taste, nor condemn him, if we are just, for knowing so human a passion," he expresses an ultimate unbelief.

For what would be the plight of a lover, if we told him that his passion was charming?—though, of course, there might be no such lady as the one he loved.[24]

Yet I do not wish to end on what may seem a note of complacent superiority. I do not think we have come any nearer to a solution of our original problem about the supernatural and how it is known; in fact I think the problem has been only intensified. We have learned, perhaps, that God is not without, but we have also learned that it is inadequate to say that he is merely within, for he is also without . . . in some sense. . . . But in what sense? We have seen that to take religious knowledge as literally true is impossible, yet to assign to it merely symbolic value is disastrous for religion. Religion must have some literal truth. But what is that truth to be? To these questions we have found no answers. We have opposing theories, and we can see that there is truth in each, but how to harmonize these truths has proved a task beyond our powers.

CHAPTER V

NATURALIZING THE SUPERNATURAL: DURKHEIM AND THE SOCIOLOGICAL HUMANISTS

IN the use of symbols there are two directions: the familiar may be used to symbolize the unfamiliar, or the unfamiliar to symbolize the familiar. Religious language frequently uses symbols in the former sense, as when parables are used to convey subtle moral truths. But for our symbolical theorists, religion makes its chief use of symbols in the opposite direction: the supernatural is used to indicate the natural. The imaginative image renders salient some strand of common experience: thus, the legend of the Fall and of the expulsion from Eden may be an elaborate dramatic rendering of the natural consequence of moral failure. By such interpretations, the supernatural becomes naturalized.

Our own inquiry into the nature of religion has made the supernatural central to it; and the attempts so far considered to evade the dilemma of religious knowledge by reducing the supernatural to the human or the psychological are dismissed as over-simplifying the problem. It is true, we have not defined the supernatural; and the term as here used may be in essence indefinable. But let me say that we do not mean by supernatural what is very often meant, "a power which mysteriously overrides and overturns the best founded human expectations."[1] An event may be unforeseen and exceptional without being supernatural in our sense: and the supernatural need not bear the character of interruption. Thus, the peculiar gift of religion, salvation with its attendant "bliss," is supernatural not because it breaks through some familiar sequence or causes surprise, but because it is irreducible to gifts of the natural order. The supernatural is a veritable factor in experience, and one which the mind can identify and grasp without being able to express. Its nature eludes rational comprehension.

To insist on the supernatural as central in religion, however, is to insist on our dilemma, a position which to many minds is intrinsically unsatisfactory. In the first place, there is something arbitrary in setting up a boundary which reason may not pass. Reason is reluctant to admit that there is any territory forbidden to her which she may not enter and subdue, and she will not surrender without a struggle what seem to be legitimate ambitions. Secondly, to call anything superrational seems dangerously like calling it antirational, and the consequences of this are not lightly to be accepted. They are, for the life of thought, superstition, emotionalism, or the cult of some vacant contemplation of the Unutterable; and for conduct, an insensate asceticism, or the heats of a fanatical idealism which would sacrifice concrete human good to some abstract and impersonal "values." No theory of religion is tolerable which brings these results in its train. The question, therefore, appears in sharper definition, whether religion may not be retained both in theory and in fact without recourse to this concept of the supernatural. Is it not possible to discover *natural equivalents* for God, for Salvation, for Miracle, and the rest, so that we may see in religion a form of the life of reason instead of playing into the hands of those who would denominate it an aberration from sanity?

In our own time a way has been found to give definite fulfilment to the hope thus intimated. The study of the history of religions and the study of Kulturgeschichte have seemed to establish two things: first, that religion instead of being a mysterious visitation of the superhuman is "a natural, social, cultural process";[2] second, that the divine is everywhere dependent on human habits and interests, and indeed may be said to reflect them. The term God, therefore, becomes susceptible of a strictly empirical meaning. It turns out, for example, that in primitive societies the bewildering variety of things that are called sacred have this in common: they are all directly or indirectly necessary to the preservation of life and particularly the life of the social group. Thus, in their several ways, they reflect the economic, the political, and the moral values of the group. In the later stages of religion the same thing holds good. Professor Ames writes:

The lesser gods, and the great gods of all religions, are seen to be the life process itself, idealized and personified. Every god bears the marks of the habits and moral character of his worshippers, and he undergoes the changes and transformations that profoundly affect his people. When they are militant, so is he; when they are peaceful, so is he; when they have a monarchy, he is a monarch; when they become democratic, he becomes friendly, renounces external authority and rules by reason and justice. God is thus shown to be the Spirit of a people, and in so far as there is a world of humanity, God is the spirit of the world.[3]

Here then is a relatively novel way of naturalizing the supernatural: religion is a purely social phenomenon and God is the Spirit of the Group. This is the theory which I now propose to examine. It is a theory which has won many followers in America today, but I prefer to study it in the work of one of its earliest and most eminent exponents, the French sociologist, Durkheim.

In a general way, writes Durkheim, "it is unquestionable that a society has all that is necessary to arouse the sensation of the divine in minds, merely by the power that it has over them; for to its members it is what a god is to his worshippers."[4] "Religious force is only the sentiment inspired by the group in its members, but projected outside of the consciousnesses that experience them, and objectified."[5] If we are looking for an analogy to the kind of process that Durkheim has in mind we can discover one in the workings of national sentiment today. The love of country is a love for the things that have made us: it is mindful of the rock from which we were hewn and the pit whence we were digged. Our national tongue, our manners and customs, our traditions, our achievements in law or in government, in art or in science—these constitute a heritage in which we share and without which the individual would be a pathetic and solitary figure devoid of definiteness and significant character. One's country is more than this. As the actually existing organization of one's fellow citizens, it provides a social environment on which from moment to moment one depends. The economic dependence is obvious: the mental dependence is less obvious but no less real. The substance of one's thoughts, the ability to express them, the specific form that one imposes on them, their direction, and their momentum—all these are in large part conferred by society. Lastly, one's country is something which exists in aspiration and ideal as well as in tradition and present fact. To feel the pulse of the national ambition beating in one's blood is to experience a generous excitement, to achieve a new perspective, to see one's own life and effort transformed by the glamor of a new range of imagination.

At those times when the national life becomes intense, these feelings of solidarity, these "collective sentiments," as Durkheim calls them, come vividly before the mind and take on an invigorated reality. One's country begins to emerge as "the national being," a transcendent power that is personified in anthems, in hymns, and in national appeals. As the power which in truth has made us and upon which we depend, it issues commands, imposes claims upon us, and everywhere speaks with the voice of authority. For those who in mystical fashion yield themselves to its immense and swiftly moving current it brings an increment of power and sets free unsuspected forces of heroism and devotion. But sentiment and passion cannot be sustained on abstractions. Some emblem for one's country must be found, some symbol, literal, vivid, accessible to all, which will focus the imagination. A flag is chosen, and since upon it are concentrated all those mysterious and potent feelings which make up the passion of patriotism, it becomes as sacred as the feelings themselves.

This brief description of the workings of the patriotic spirit contains in epitome the story of the origin* and nature of religion. Let us look at the story more closely.

If we take the term "God" or "the Divine" in its most general sense we discover in it the following elements:

(1) A power greater than and external to the believer, on which he depends.

(2) A power which imposes on the believer claims, both positive and negative, which have no manifest connection with utility.

(3) The god speaks with authority: his commands inspire *respect*.

(4) Man can enter into communion with the divine. The results are a sense of exaltation, increased confidence and power.

(5) The divine is "sacred," "holy," as contrasted

---

* I use the word "origin" subject to Durkheim's reservation. "If by origin we are to understand the very first beginning, the question has nothing scientific about it, and should be discarded. There was no given moment when religion began to exist. . . . Like every human institution, religion did not commence anywhere" (*Elementary Forms, etc.,* p. 8).

with the profane—"two classes which embrace all that exists, but which radically exclude each other."*

Now society satisfies all these conditions.

(1) "Society also gives us the sensation of a continual dependence."⁶ "The believer . . . believes in the existence of a moral power upon which he depends . . . this power exists, it is society."⁷

(2) "Since it [society] has a nature which is peculiar to itself and different from our individual nature, it pursues ends which are likewise special to it; but, as it cannot attain them except through our intermediacy, it imperiously demands our aid. It requires that, forgetful of our own interests, we make ourselves its servitors, and it submits us to every sort of privation and sacrifice, without which social life would be impossible. It is because of this that at every instant we are obliged to submit ourselves to rules of conduct and of thought which we have neither made nor desired, and which are sometimes even contrary to our most fundamental inclinations and instincts."⁸

(3) "But if we yield to its [society's] orders, it is not merely because it is strong enough to triumph over our resistance; it is primarily because it is the object of a venerable respect. . . . Now the ways of action to which society is strongly enough attached to impose them upon its members are, by that very fact, marked with a distinctive sign provocative of respect.

* *Elementary Forms, etc.,* p. 40. Cf. also, "The sacred character assumed by an object is not implied in the intrinsic properties of this latter: it is added to them. The world of religious things is not one particular aspect of empirical nature: it is superimposed upon it" (p. 229).

Since they are elaborated in common, the vigour with which they have been thought of by each particular mind is retained in all the other minds, and reciprocally. . . . So opinion, primarily a social thing, is a source of authority. . . ."[9]

(4) "The collective force is not entirely outside of us; it does not act upon us wholly from without; but rather, since society cannot exist except in and through individual consciousnesses, this force must also penetrate us and organize itself within us; it thus becomes an integral force of our being and by that very fact this is elevated and magnified."[10] "The man who is in moral harmony with his comrades, has more confidence, courage and boldness in action, just like the believer who thinks that he feels the regard of his god turned graciously towards him."[11] "When the Australian is carried outside himself and feels a new life flowing within him whose intensity surprises him, he is not the dupe of an illusion; this exaltation is real and is really the effect of forces outside of and superior to the individual."[12]

(5) A flag, considered in itself, as a piece of colored cloth, inspires only "ordinary" sentiments, but considered as an embodiment of social forces it is a consecrated symbol of extraordinary potency. It is society that thus creates sacred things out of ordinary ones.[13]
"The simple deference inspired by men invested with high social functions is not different in nature from religious respect. It is expressed by the same movements: a man keeps at a distance from a high personage; he approaches him only with precautions; in

conversing with him he uses other gestures and language than those used with ordinary mortals."[14] "Thus the environment in which we live seems to us to be peopled with forces that are at once imperious and helpful, august and gracious, and with which we have relations. Since they exercise over us a pressure of which we are conscious, we are forced to localize them outside our natures, just as we do for the objective cause of our sensations. But the sentiments which they inspire in us differ in nature from those which we have for simple visible objects. As long as these latter are reduced to their empirical characteristics as shown in ordinary experience, and as long as the religious imagination has not metamorphosed them, we entertain for them no feeling which resembles respect, and they contain nothing that is able to raise us outside ourselves. Therefore, the representations which express them appear to us to be very different from those aroused in us by collective influences. The two form two distinct and separate states in our consciousness, just as the two forms of life to which they correspond. Consequently, we get the impression that we are in relations with two distinct sorts of reality and that a sharply drawn line of demarcation separates them from each other: on the one hand is the world of profane things, on the other, that of sacred things."[15]

This theory, Durkheim contended, explains the apparent arbitrariness which religion has shown in those things it has chosen to call sacred.

The lizard, the caterpillar, the rat, the ant, the frog, the turkey, the fish, the plum-tree, the cockatoo, etc., to cite only those names which occur frequently in the lists of Australian totems, are not of a nature to produce upon men those great and strong impressions which in a way resemble religious emotions and which impress a sacred character upon the objects they create.[16]

The totem is the emblem of the group: it is the clan itself "personified and represented to the imagination" in a material symbol. The choice of symbol will, of course, depend on accident of local circumstance or custom, and the variety of symbolic objects will be correspondingly great.

The foregoing sketch may serve as a reminder of the most general features of the theory of religion proposed by sociology. As I have not presented it in detail I shall not attempt to criticize it in detail. I shall confine myself to pointing out and examining two ambiguities in the sociologist's account. The first turns upon the meaning of the term "society"; the second on the answer to the question, Is religion truth or illusion?

The theory prides itself above all on being scientific. Society, we are told, is a real object, whose structure and functions lie open to empirical observation and study. It is a fact of the natural order, with nothing transcendental or supernatural about it. And if God is simply another name for society or the spirit of the group then religion will have been successfully naturalized and many of its traditional puzzles will vanish.

What then is society as here described? To begin

with, it is admittedly not the same as the members of any one group existing at any one period of time. It is not even the same as the aggregate of human beings existing at any one time and labeled humanity. For society includes those who are dead. The great social power upon which men feel themselves continuously dependent, of which they become intensely conscious at times of social excitement or on occasions of solemn public observance, is embodied much less in the group of their fellow members than in those nameless and invisible generations whose achievements they inherit.

We speak [as Durkheim says] a language that we did not make; we use instruments that we did not invent; we invoke rights that we did not found; a treasury of knowledge is transmitted to each generation that it did not gather itself, etc. It is to society that we owe these various benefits of civilization. . . .[17]

My question is, Does *this* society exist in any verifiable sense? Of course it is true that every man inherits a culture and a civilization which he did not make, but simply finds. But we are not justified in going beyond these facts and invoking a thing called Society as their cause and explanation. The appeal to Society, rather than to more obviously natural factors to explain so-called social inheritance, involves the hypothesis that there has been a unity of social life and a continuity of social purpose throughout the centuries. This hypothesis is consistent with the facts, but it is not necessary and, in the nature of things, it cannot be verified. Society, in short, as Durkheim uses the term, is not an object of scientific study at all; it is a mystical entity whose life pervades and unifies successive generations.

The conclusion is confirmed when we look at the situation from a different point of view. One of the first objections that comes to mind when it is proposed to substitute Society for God is that any actual human society, however civilized, is too undiscriminating in its judgments, too impersonal in its methods, too ignorant and too cruel, to serve as an object of worship.

The real society [says Durkheim] such as it is and acts before our eyes . . . is full of defects and imperfections. . . . How could anything so crudely organised inspire the sentiments of love, the ardent enthusiasm, and the spirit of abnegation which all religions claim of their followers. These perfect beings which are gods could not have taken their traits from so mediocre, and sometimes even so base a reality.[18]

No, the society to which religion directs its worship is an ideal society which it sets over against the actual and tries to realize. We have therefore to ask the same question about this possible future society as we asked about the vanished society of the past, Does it exist? Actual society won't do for religion—possible society won't do for science.

The difficulty is crucial, and Durkheim's way of meeting it is instructive. He points out that for the successful conduct of individual life there should be periods devoted to the deepening of self-consciousness and the recovery of the sense of direction. In the same way, society finds it necessary from time to time to "assemble and concentrate itself." At such times "collective forces" come into existence and produce a general heightening of social consciousness. The consequent "exaltation of the mental life . . . takes form in a group of ideal conceptions where is portrayed the new life thus awakened."[19] "A society can neither create itself nor recreate itself without at the same time creating an ideal."[20] Durkheim is here calling attention to a perfectly familiar phenomenon that we can observe daily, the way that societies have of reminding themselves by appropriate ceremonies of their purposes, of their aspirations, and in general of the things they stand for. It is natural, we might say, for any group to form an ideal of itself. From this Durkheim draws the astonishing conclusion that the ideal is a natural fact. "The formation of the ideal world," he writes, "is therefore not an irreducible fact which escapes science; it depends upon conditions which observation can touch; it is a natural product of social life."[21]

By thus including in the definition of society "the faculty of idealising," so that the ideal society may be said to be "a part of the real society," Durkheim seems to have answered the gravest objection to which his type of theory has been exposed. For all attempts to explain morality or religion as the echo in the individual mind of social commands or as the regimentation imposed by social custom have found it hard to explain how the individual comes to be the growing point of morality and religion. Conscience often requires a man to protest quite sincerely against public opinion in the name of some moral insight, and, historically, it has been the function of the nonconformist to raise the level of social judgment.* In the same way, the mystic and the prophet have shown an originality proportionate to their detachment from the forces of social gravitation, while the unmistakable tendency of religion is toward a spiritual individualism. If anything makes one sincere, fearless, and superior to social standards it is religion. Thus James writes of Tolstoy after the period of his conversion:

> His later works show him implacable to the whole system of official values: the ignobility of fashionable life; the infamies of empire; the spuriousness of the Church; the vain conceit of the professions; the meannesses and cruelties that go with great success; and every other pompous crime and lying institution of the world. To all patience with such things his experience has been a permanent ministry of death.[22]

But if religion and morality, to which this attitude is native, are social derivatives, how can society have turned thus against itself? That has been the question persistently addressed to sociologists.

Now Durkheim's contention that it is characteristic of a society to form an ideal picture of its function and destiny seems, as I said, to meet this difficulty. For it is "at the school of collective life that the individual† has learned to idealise."[23] If society were merely a

---

* For a sociological explanation of Conscience, see Paulsen, *A System of Ethics,* Eng. trans., pp. 363 ff., and for a criticism, A. K. Rogers, *Theory of Ethics,* pp. 58 f.

† Why the individual should need to *learn* this is not made clear. "It is irrelevant to deny, as M. Durkheim does, a mystic faculty of idealisation, for it is not at all mystical, nor is it a special faculty. It is, on the contrary, the normal counterpart to the judgment of the fact" (J. M. Baldwin, *Genetic Theory of Reality,* p. 115, n. 2).

part of the natural environment then we could not explain the presence in the individual of the "idealising
faculty," for you cannot derive the ideal from the natural, the "ought to be" from the "is." But society has
ideals and can communicate them to its members. "It
is in assimilating the ideals elaborated by society that
the individual has become capable of conceiving the
ideal."[24]

Let me set down briefly the difficulties that I find
in this account. First, to assimilate ideals is not the
same as to acquire "the faculty of idealising." In fact,
the former presupposes the latter. The corporate loyalty
or enthusiasm which the members of a group acquire
through imitation or under the influence of social suggestion is not strictly speaking idealism at all; it may
be as devoid of moral quality as the surrender to mob
spirit or to the fascination of "keeping step." For an
ideal to be accepted as such, something more is necessary than to have it presented or imposed. The feeling
for the ideal and the willingness to adopt it must first
be evoked. In other words the individual cannot assimilate an ideal unless he possesses just that "vague
innate power" which Durkheim denies to him.

Leaving aside this difficulty there are others more
serious. I think we may fairly say that Durkheim, instead of solving the problem of the status of the ideal
world, has simply transferred it from the individual to
society. For he nowhere explains how the ideal society
can be regarded as "part of the real society." Real society, we must remember, is here taken as natural
empirical fact. To say that "the formation of the ideal

world depends upon conditions which observation can touch" and "is a natural product of social life," is not to show that ideals are facts of the natural order. It simply means that we can observe the rise and play of ideal forces; but to say that we can see a thing happening is not to say that we understand *how* it happens. That, indeed, is something which the sociologist is forced to leave mysterious, and it is strange that Durkheim fails to see how he surrenders the very center of his position when he writes, "A society is not made up merely of the mass of individuals who compose it, . . . but above all *is the idea which it forms of itself.*"[25] For this amounts to saying that society possesses a "vague innate power" of idealizing. But if society may be supposed to have this faculty there is no reason why the individual may not be similarly endowed, and consequently no need to trace his aptitude to a social origin. In other words, if you don't have to explain how society can have access to the ideal world, why do you have to provide an explanation for the individual's access to that world? If the religion of society can be taken for granted, why cannot the religion of the individual be taken for granted instead of regarding it as communicated to him by society?

Consider now some further consequences of this admission that "society is the idea which it forms of itself," that, in the happy phrase of Boutroux, "Society is not an object, but a subject." Society, let us now agree, in its ideal aspect and function, does not exist as an object of scientific study. That Great Being which positivism asks men to serve and to worship by separate acts of justice, kindness, and loyalty, to their fellows, does not exist. Society may be unified at some future time; it is not unified yet. It may be perfected at some future time; it is not perfect yet. Society is not a thing already made; it is something in the making. It exists more in the region of will and aspiration than in that of actuality. Society, in short, is beyond society as man is beyond man. And now we must add that it draws its life from its hold on this "beyond." Whatever unity, solidarity, and moral perfection society may claim as actual present accomplishment is a fruit of devotion to that vaguely conceived ideal. I have found this no-where more strikingly expressed than in the following passage from a book by Professor Jacks.

. . . The kind of welfare that society achieves by concen-trating attention on its own welfare, as the only thing that really matters, is bound to be second-rate and poverty-stricken. That individual selfishness is self-defeating nobody needs to be told. No human society has ever prospered, or ever can prosper, by concentrating exclusive attention on its own welfare. Without a certain indifference to its own welfare, without a certain capacity for forgetting all about it in the pursuit of something greater, the life of society, even if inter-national, is bound to be shallow and miserable; while society itself, considered as having no function but to exploit the universe for its own advantage, stands out in colors which can only be described as morally despicable.

The best things human society enjoys at this moment are the result of efforts which have *not* had the welfare of so-ciety for their object; while of the worst evils not a few can be directly traced to its corporate selfishness—to its lack of reverence for anything but itself. Social selfishness in morality, like institutional selfishness in religion, acts as a deadly stranglehold on the spirit of man.

Of the goods possessed by society the best are religion, philosophy, science, and art. These are not the products of the entire human class consciousness, absorbingly concentrated on the welfare of society. The human class consciousness is fatal to them. They flourish only in minds which have risen above it.[26]

In other words, the service or worship of humanity that is fruitful is never merely a service of humanity as a contemporary fact, but the service of something beyond humanity, by aspiring after which generations, past, present, and future, help to build the perfect society. Unless our humanitarian ambition succeeds in establishing connections with this "beyond," it loses all force and significance.

Thus after this tedious analysis and criticism we have come again upon this mysterious "beyond"—this time in the form of a supersocial good which religion grasps but does not define. The attempt therefore to substitute objects at once social and natural for the transcendental objects of religion must, I think, be called a failure. Society, it seems, if it is to serve as an equivalent for God, must in some sense possess those very attributes which caused so much difficulty in the conception of God supernaturally conceived. Religion proves to be occupied with some supersocial good which is irreducible to the social goods recognized at any particular stage of society's development.

I said at the beginning of this discussion that w'

should confine our treatment to two questions: one concerning the origin and nature of religion as interpreted by sociology, the other concerning its truth. Having disposed of the first to the best of our ability we now turn to a consideration of the second.

Durkheim repeatedly insists that "it is an essential postulate of sociology that a human institution cannot rest upon an error and a lie. . . . If it were not founded on the nature of things it would have encountered in the facts a resistance over which it could not have triumphed."[27] Statements of this kind naturally lead us to expect that religion will be shown to be something more than the record of social forces, and that the belief in God, for example—the belief in "a being whom men think of as superior to themselves, and upon whom they feel that they depend"[28]—is not illusory, but *bien fondu.* As soon, however, as we begin to inquire what foundation of truth is meant, we are assailed by perplexity. For we recall such statements as "the god and the society are one,"[29] and, "religious representations are collective representations which express collective realities,"[30] and these surely mean that God, in the sense in which religion uses the term, does not really exist, and that religious beliefs are illusions generated by social needs.

The apparent inconsistency may perhaps disappear if we draw a distinction between the truth of the individual's beliefs and the truth of society's beliefs. Of the former we must say, not that they are false, but that they are symbolically true. For consider. The individual believes that he is dependent on a higher power external to himself. He is right: that power is society. He believes that by identifying himself with it he can add to his own vital energies. He is right: he gets an increase of power from participating in the life of his group. He believes that this power requires him to do or to refrain from doing certain things. Again, he is right; but this pressure is social in origin.[31] Now "social life in all its aspects, and in every period of its history, is made possible only by a vast symbolism."[32] Thus one personifies the group under the figure of Alma Mater or of "My Country"; one personifies Justice; one talks of "the national honor"; the soil is sacred, or the flag is sacred, and so on. The only error the individual makes is in taking these symbols for literal truth, in thinking that the power resides in or comes from the sacred object or from some divine being behind it. Now the question whether the individual is ultimately deceived or not cannot be decided until we have looked more closely at this vast symbolism and the collective representations from which it takes its rise. Pursuing this line of inquiry, we discover that

religious force is only the sentiment inspired by the group in its members, but projected outside of the consciousnesses that experience them, and objectified. . . . The sacred character assumed by an object is not implied in the intrinsic properties of this latter: it is added to them.[33]

That is, to take Durkheim's favorite example, the flag is not *really* sacred. Intrinsically, it is only a piece of colored cloth. But the collective imagination seizes upon this and sanctifies it, so as to make it the means of strengthening and perpetuating the life of the group. But what is this if not to say that the world is not *really* divine? The real world is the world as the common experience of the individual presents it. The quality of divinity is something imported into it under the influence of collective excitement, and religion, therefore, *from the point of view of the sociologist who has seen through its pretensions,* must be described as a collective hallucination. And if the collective mind is deceived the mind of the individual shares in the deception.

Now this is a conclusion which Durkheim specifically rejects. In order to see how he attempts to justify himself, we may profitably glance for a moment at his treatment of the corresponding difficulty in the doctrine of the categories. The categories are explained as products of the collective mind, and their necessity and authority are ultimately traced to the operation of social forces. Their authority "is the very authority of society, transferring itself to a certain manner of thought which is the indispensable condition of all communication."* Without the concepts of time, of space, and of causation, for example, social life would be impossible. From this point of view, then, the necessity of these forms of thought is ultimately practical, and their truth is constituted by social agreement. But the criticism immediately occurs to us: If the categories are merely social conveniences, then their authority is

---

* A few lines before Durkheim explains the necessity thus, "If our whole thought is not to cease being really human." But this condition is not imposed by society: it is imposed by an ideal—the ideal of being human. P. 17.

binding only on those who are socially inclined; they contain no finally compelling necessity. And to this we must add that truth cannot be determined by social agreement: social agreement must rest on truth.* Now Durkheim feels the force of this objection, and he meets it by saying that the categories are not merely social constructs, but "are not without foundation in the nature of things. . . . They are, in a sense, a work of art, but of an art which imitates nature with a perfection capable of increasing unlimitedly."[34] Durkheim does not elaborate this idea, but his meaning can only be that in the last analysis the authority of the categories is derived from their correspondence with fact.

He adopts the same line of argument when he comes to those collective representations which constitute the objects and beliefs of religion. To exhibit the social origins of these, he says, is not to show that they "are devoid of all objective value," but rather to show that "they are not without foundation in the nature of things."[35] It is difficult to discover what in detail these words mean, but in general it is clear that they amount to an admission that "the nature of reality reflects itself in the constitution of society," and that, in consequence, religion confers "a genuine apprehension of a reality which escapes the purview alike of the senses and of the natural sciences."[36] Religion, that is, takes man out into worlds of reality and of truth which lie beyond society—a strange conclusion for a theory which set out to exhibit religion as a purely social phenomenon!

* For Durkheim's account of this objection, see p. 437.

Yet in the light of the ambiguities in the concept of society this result can hardly surprise us. If society was to possess the functions attributed to it by the sociologists then society had to be more than a natural fact: it had to be an entity the very essence of which included a prophetic grasp of some supersocial ideal. And so when we examine those beliefs upon which religion lives, we find that they are not symbolic translations of natural social forces, but rather intimations of forces truly cosmic in sweep. Yet these forces, like the supersocial good, "escape the purview of the senses and of the natural sciences." However fine the net of definition and however close we draw it, these slip back into the waters of the "beyond."

I conclude, therefore, that the sociological theory of religion is as little able to rescue us from our original predicament as any of the other theories we have examined. This bold attempt to naturalize the supernatural only serves to give fresh emphasis to the problem: Reason cannot do with the supernatural, and Religion cannot do without it.

CHAPTER VI

SUFFOCATION IN THE SUBCONSCIOUS: FREUD AND THE PSYCHOLOGISTS

OUR meditations tend toward a general result: The claim of faith to apprehend objective reality maintains itself as fundamental to religion. In other words, the concept of divine revelation as something given from outside to the spiritual sense, proves critical for the understanding of religion. Yet we have in no way canceled the difficulty in the idea of an apparition or intervention of God from without. We have examined several representative attempts to transform this idea in such way as to emancipate religion from error and contradiction. All these undertakings have had a common complexion: they all offered a revised version of the validity of religious doctrine, making religious expression essentially symbolic. Instead of telling literal truth about a supernatural order, what religion reveals is truth about human nature and its aspirations. Thus for "the God that is without" was substituted "the God that is within," whether within the human mind or within the social order. But we have still to examine one further attempt to find a natural equivalent for the supernatural. We are to ask how far what psychology has to tell us about the subconscious provides a solution of our problem.

Psychologists, of course, are far from being agreed

on any one theory of the origin or of the mode of operation of the subconscious; but if they admit its existence at all, they regard it as part of the natural human equipment (either original or acquired) to be described and explained in terms of verifiable psychological laws. To show that any phenomenon is derived from the subconscious is therefore to ascribe to it a natural as contrasted with a supernatural origin. Now, as is well known, this is just the kind of explanation that has in recent years been brought with apparent success to many of the phenomena of religion. Inspiration, revelation, the feelings of dependence on, and control by, an external power—these and many others can be matched in secular or nonreligious experience where a purely natural explanation seems possible and sufficient. If we do not invoke a supernatural cause to explain, for example, poetic inspiration, we should not and need not appeal to the supernatural to explain religious inspiration. In the subconscious we are presented with the idea of a division of the mind into sections or stories. These different levels of mental life may prove to correspond to the religious distinction between inner and outer, and the intervention of God is perhaps to be described as the intervention of the subconscious. Clearly, if this program could be carried out we should realize that belief in the supernatural was due to ignorance of the subconscious and of its workings, and we should have found in the subconscious a natural equivalent for the supernatural.

The term "subconscious," as I have just said, implies that the mind is divided into two parts, a conscious part and a subconscious part; or, to express the thing in a less controversial way, that there are two kinds of mental process, conscious mental process and subconscious mental process. It will simplify our procedure if we begin by asking what reasons have led psychologists to make this distinction. What facts have led them to postulate a subconscious? What is the evidence for its existence?

Although most of the evidence has, as a matter of fact, been furnished in our own time by the study of abnormal subjects, I prefer to take first some normal phenomena.

(1) You are sitting in your room reading. The noise of traffic in the street is continuous; but you are not "consciously aware" of it. The noise ceases. You become aware of this. But how could you notice an interruption unless you had been previously aware of that which is interrupted? Thus, in some mysterious way, you were aware and not aware.

(2) In the exercise of any acquired skill—such as playing a piece of music we are familiar with—we *use* much knowledge that we do not consciously *attend* to. The knowledge is *in* the mind, but not *before* it.

(3) Desire—a mental process—notoriously influences much thought and conduct without our being aware of it.

(4) A hypnotized subject is given a problem in arithmetic and told to have the solution ready in two hours' time. He is then immediately awakened. He remembers nothing of the instructions given to him. At the appointed time he produces the solution. The operation

involved is evidently mental, yet the subject has not performed it consciously.

(5) A patient suffering from some distressing neurosis consults a psychoanalyst who traces the trouble to some event that happened years ago and which the patient had completely forgotten. The memory of the incident, together with its associations, had been in the patient's mind all that time: they had influenced his thought and his conduct; but he had been unaware of their presence.

(6) According to the Freudian theory, the dream is the fulfilment of a suppressed wish. The literal fulfilment of the wish would shock us into wakefulness. The so-called censor prohibits this. The wish then sets about to find its satisfaction indirectly. The result is the dream—a figurative fulfilment of the wish which outwits the censor. You thus have two processes which are mental in character: first, the wish seeking fulfilment; second, the ingenious symbolical construction of the dream. Both of these are, as we must say, "unconscious."

The above list makes no pretense to be exhaustive. Some important items, such as the phenomena of radical dissociation, have been omitted; some items have been included that hardly seem to call for explanation in terms of the subconscious at all. But, incomplete as it is, the list will serve to reveal a character that all subconscious phenomena possess. That character is what I may call, if the expression is allowed, "in-and-outness." The sensation, the acquired knowledge, the desire, the memory, the repressed wish, and so forth, are plainly *in* the mind: they exert an influence there, and they are in principle, if not always in fact, accessible to the mind and may be recognized as belonging to it. Yet, although they are *in* the mind, they are not *before* it, and they may have an air that is so strange and even foreign that they can be said to be *outside* the mind. Yet how can something be at once inside the mind and outside it? The obvious device for naming, if not for explaining, this paradox, is to divide the mind. We make a distinction between consciousness and subconsciousness, and we assign the mysterious phenomena to the latter.

So far—apart from problematical cases of complete dissociation—there is nothing to justify the idea of any radical sundering of the mind. But we can hardly deny that both psychologists and laymen often talk of the subconscious as though it were *a separate place in the mind,* or *a separate mysterious self* within each of us. An illustration of the former may be found in a familiar objection to the use of the subconscious as an explanation of religious experiences. It is said that there is something degrading in the thought that God should enter the soul by a channel rendered so malodorous by the unsavory ancestral or bestial impulses that move along it. We should look, we are told, for the revelation of God, not by way of the sedimentary depths, but in the higher rational, moral, and aesthetic experiences. This kind of criticism plainly implies that the critic is thinking of the subconscious as a separate *place* in the mind, as a sort of special mental duct or sewer. Freud, on the other hand, makes us think of the subconscious not as a separate place but almost as a separate self, a being with enough personality to build the elaborate and cunning structures of dream, and to disturb the equanimity and the self-respect of the conscious self by unwanted interruptions. Now I do not believe that there is anything in the evidence to justify this splitting of the mind into two parts or two selves; even in abnormal cases I think we have nothing more than extreme examples of a perfectly normal phenomenon, the fluctuation of the mind's power of attention. How, then, do we come so readily to believe that there are *two minds:* "the conscious mind" and "the subconscious mind"? Why is it so fatally easy to substitute "a division *of* the mind" for "a division *in* the mind"?

The chief factor, I think, is the influence of spatial imagery. Recall some of the images most frequently used to illuminate the relation between subconscious and conscious. The submerged seven-eighths of the iceberg and the one-eighth above water; the wide body of the bottle and the narrow neck; the reservoir or the storehouse which overflows; the seed germinating in the soil and then sprouting into the air; the antechamber;* the penumbra and focus. We cannot well

* "We will compare the system of the unconscious to a large antechamber, in which the psychic impulses rub elbows with one another, as separate beings. There opens out of this antechamber another, a smaller room, a sort of parlor, which consciousness occupies. But on the threshold between the two rooms there stands a watchman; he passes on the individual psychic impulses, censors them, and will not let them into the parlor if they do not meet with his approval. . . . I know they [these conceptions] are crude—indeed we even know that they are incorrect. . . . For the time being, they are useful conceptions. . . . I should like to assure you that these crude assumptions go far in approximating the actual situation. . . ." Sigmund Freud, *A General Introduction to Psychoanalysis,* trans. G. Stanley Hall, 11th ed., pp. 256 f.

dispense with such pictures, but one result of using them is to impose the separateness of spatial relation upon our thinking, and so to produce the conception of the subconscious as a separate place in the mind—a mental *region from* which impulses or ideas or desires pass *into* the conscious mind. One example will suffice to show the falsification thus introduced into our account of mental process. You compare, let us say, the subconscious to the margin and the conscious to the focus of attention. You have a center of light fixed in one place, surrounded by an area of shadow. Notice that in comparing the mind to a field of attention you have destroyed the mind's activity. The mind now is a passive field or stage. But things go on in the mind; dramas are enacted there. How, in terms of our figure, are we to describe this? Evidently we shall have to confer on the different items of mental life—the ideas, desires, feelings, complexes, and so on—a sort of active existence of their own. We shall have to treat them as characters which pass from the wings to the stage and back again. From time to time in our study of mental life we shall be confronted with this question: Why does such and such an impulse leave the subconscious, the dimly lighted region, and enter the conscious, the clearly lighted focus? We can only answer by assuming that this impulse has a sort of power of psychic motion of its own, that it is, in a word, a sort of miniature self. And this, I submit, is mythology, not science. It is the now discredited psychology of "mental chemistry" in disguise. Discredited, because complexes, ideas, wishes, and so forth, are not separate mental entities or forces.

The whole source of the trouble is to be found in that original metaphor—the field of attention. A field is a passive thing: a field does not attend to itself. But the mind has the power of attending. In comparing the mind to a field, what you have done is to take this integral attentive activity of the mind and dissipate it into a number of separate activities which you bestow on the separate mental items, complexes, and the rest. If, however, we remember that the mind is attentive and self-active, then our problem is, "Why does the mind attend to certain things and not to others?" instead of the impossible problem, "Why do certain psychic entities pass from the margin to the center of the field of attention?"

I propose, therefore, to go behind the unfortunate assumptions of picture thinking and to propound two questions: (1) How much truth is there in the idea of a division *of* the mind? (2) How are we to explain such transactions as are described in the familiar phrase, "an uprush from the subconscious"?

(1) We may note first that the technique of psychoanalysis presupposes a potential unity of the mind. It is precisely this unity which the psychoanalyst is trying to restore. Even with the most extreme cases of dissociation, there is nothing, in principle, to forbid the psychoanalyst from hoping to integrate the mind of the patient. The patient, in any event, has to coöperate with the doctor: what both are working for is to put the patient *in possession of himself*. The reply may be that the doctor creates, rather than restores, unity. A unified

mind, we may be told, is an ideal: we are all more or less "dissociated," as we all fall short of sanity. From this point of view, the work of the psychoanalyst would be the construction of a "self" out of fragments, not a reconstruction. But this is hardly compatible with the technique itself. We will suppose, for example, that the treatment at some stage is designed to help the patient to recall some long-forgotten incident in his past life, or to acknowledge some unpleasant truth about his own impulses. Clearly there is an assumption here that there is in the patient a consciousness which can include the present situation and the for-gotten incident within one act of recognition, that there is a self which can face all the truth, pleasant and unpleasant, about its impulses. This unitary conscious-ness or self is not constructed by the psychoanalyst: it is something that he is trying to *arouse*. The working assumptions of psychoanalysis as an art, therefore, point to a unity of consciousness which goes deeper than any division.

The same fact will appear if we look again for a moment at that list of similes—iceberg, bottle, and the rest. These spell continuity. Just as liquid can pass up from the body of the bottle into the neck and down from the neck into the bottle, so there is give-and-take between subconsciousness and consciousness. Even where the figure employed most obviously suggests compartments and sundering walls, one no sooner says "wall" than one cancels the exclusiveness implied. I am thinking of Freud's censor[1] who stands guard at the door leading from the antechamber of the subconscious to the front room of the conscious.* The censor is admittedly a symbolic figure,[2] but he stands for observed facts. *And the censor is privy to what goes on in both rooms:* the censor, that is, is a name for consciousness which includes both the subconscious and the conscious. He represents the promise or vestige, whichever way you like to look at it, of that unity of the mind which lies beneath the division, of that integral activity of the mind itself which much talk of dissociation tends to obscure.

(2) Our second question is, How are we to describe a so-called "uprush from the subconscious"? We have refused to take literally the idea that a subconscious item has the sort of independent activity ascribed to it in that phrase, and we have rejected the notion that the subconscious is a sort of reservoir that at times becomes so full that it overflows. What language then do we propose to use? Let us take a relatively simple example of the kind of experience referred to.

Here is a man whom I know well. I like him and trust him. Then on one or two occasions when talking with him I find myself aware of a slight discomfort. He does not seem to have been quite so frank as I could have wished. On reflection, I decide that these are unworthy suspicions. I try to ignore them. Then I hear

* The misleading influence of spatial imagery is again apparent. Whoever compares the mind to a house with rooms has already degraded the mind to a place. Places do not move about. Whatever movement, therefore, goes on in the mind must be assigned to the complexes, neuroses, etc., that throng its chambers. The only unity left for the mind will be that of a container, but this is not equivalent to mental unity for the simple reason that a container does not attend to its contents.

others speaking ill of him, accusing him of downright duplicity. Loyalty urges me to come to his defense. I do so, but there is a residue of uncertainty and unhappiness in my mind which, when I next meet him, makes me, half against my will, a little watchful of his manner. My new suspicions find some confirmation, but I refuse to entertain them seriously, and, of course, I do not dream of revealing them to him. So it goes: occasions for distrust multiply: many straws show which way the wind is blowing, but I still refuse to admit that I feel a draught. I will have it out neither with myself nor with him. There comes a time when I discover him in what I am sure is a deliberate deception, but even now I refuse to speak out. Perhaps I am one of those persons who intensely dislike "a scene." In the name of good form I suppress my legitimate criticisms of the man. At last he convicts himself with a lie so flagrant that there can no longer be any doubt. The time for suspended judgment, reticence, and charity is gone. The breaking point has been reached. Now I see, beyond possibility of doubt, what manner of man he is. I speak out my mind to him, and, as anger mounts, all my secret suspicions, all those feelings I had so resolutely put down, pour out in an exhilarating spate.

This little episode can readily be described in terms of the subconscious. Is it not a history of doubts and suspicions suppressed one after another from conventional motives, thrust down into the subconscious, until at last that psychic cellar became too full and its contents burst up into the conscious, submerging the barriers that had separated these two parts of the mind?

I think that any such description leaves out of account several important features of the situation. First, we may note that my suppression of criticisms introduces an element of constraint into my relations with the other person. The mere recollection of my mental reservations is enough to prevent me from being wholly frank with him. My agreement, when I agree with him, may be a little too hearty, my laughter a shade forced, or, on the point of giving him a confidence, I may suddenly hesitate. In short, as I accumulate a subconscious, I become an "unnatural" self.

Secondly, concomitant with this internal opposition, there is an external opposition. For, as the strain between us increases, I make a distinction between the man as he really is and the man as, for purposes of social politeness, I assume him to be. The unpleasant or sinister facts about him I deliberately refuse to face. Thus, while it may be true that I am retreating into the subconscious, I am at the same time retreating from reality.

Thirdly, the merging of the subconscious and the conscious, the disappearance of my "unnatural" self, when the breaking point is reached, is *at the same time* a restoration to reality. When the other man has shown himself unmistakably to be a liar, I exclaim to myself, "Farewell to self-deception: *now* I see you for the man you really are!" He is no longer for me a twofold creature, to part of whose character I have closed my eyes: I see him in his entirety.

This analysis reveals, I think, that the stage called

"the breaking point" cannot be exhaustively described as a rearrangement of psychical factors, as a mere change in the psychic pattern. For we are dealing with something more than an event in the natural history of a mind. The total event is, so to speak, two-sided. On one side it is an alteration of psychic pattern, but on the other it is "restoration to reality." Now psychology selects the former side and chooses to study it in abstraction from the latter. That is both legitimate and necessary. It is only when we take the psychologist's side as constituting the whole reality, and his descriptions as exhaustive, that the trouble begins. For we are then left with the problem of explaining these changes in psychic pattern. We have states of mind which are supposed to exist in their own right and to move by some psychic force of their own, we have neuroses which "sink" or "rise" by some mysterious psychic gravitation. The problem is to explain why they behave as they do. To this no answer can be given, for the good reason that a mythological problem cannot be solved in scientific terms.

If, however, we restore to our account that aspect which psychology neglects, then I think we may make the following assertion: Wherever you get a resolution of some mental conflict through the fusion of the conscious and the subconscious, that resolution is precipitated by the *discovery of an object* which is common object for conscious and subconscious alike.[3] Unity and integration in the self are concomitant with unity and integration in the world known by that self. I believe that this statement will hold good throughout the range of subconscious phenomena. I shall content myself with suggesting how the principle may be applied in the sphere of religious experience.

Before conversion, let us say, a man has felt "consciously wrong, inferior, and unhappy." As a result of conversion, inner harmony, peace, and confidence become an assured possession. There are two ways of describing this. On the one hand, you can say that all the man's repressed impulses to goodness and to holiness of life have now "risen from the subconscious" and taken control. There has been a rearrangement of psychic pattern, a redistribution of mental energies. On the other hand, applying the principle enunciated above, you can say that in conversion the mind has discovered an object to which that mind can expose itself, so to speak, in its entirety, without reservation. The mind has been unified because it has found an object which is common object for subconscious and conscious. Now such an object looks very like God. God is the one being in whose presence we cannot, even if we would, conceal anything: here if anywhere we are our real selves. "Almighty God unto whom all hearts be open, all desires known and from whom no secrets are hid." And my point is, that there is nothing in the first description which precludes us from adopting the second. For all that psychology has to say, conversion might be what the convert thinks it is—the soul's discovery of God. Everything psychology has to say about the subconscious, of the "slow processes of maturation" going on there and culminating in some invasion of the conscious, would still remain true within its limits. The one thing which as psychologists we could not do would be to prejudge the metaphysical issue by thinking of the subconscious as a place in the mind *from which* the saving impulses come, something that could be offered as a natural origin for so-called supernatural apparitions. In short, to say that "the subconscious did it" does not prevent one from saying "God did it." Both statements may be true at the same time. In conversion the deeps of the soul are stirred. True. But it is also true that an angel may have troubled the pool.

If our argument has been sound, then, I think we may say that we have discovered a way to avoid the prison in which psychological explanations of religion threaten to confine us. For we know now that revelation cannot be reduced to an internal transaction between parts of the mind, that we are not incarcerated within the walls of the self. The danger is one that has threatened us in every theory of religious knowledge that we have examined: all of them ended in subjectivism, tacit or confessed. I have hitherto confined myself to pointing out what I thought were the logical weaknesses. But I may as well confess that I should hardly have been so concerned to do this if my real objections had not lain deeper than the theoretical. Subjectivism is intolerable both emotionally and practically, because it reduces life to a soliloquy. We suffocate within the walls of the self: we welcome anything that promises to let in the fresh air or to lead us out into the open. And since these emotional and practical needs have determined our treatment throughout, I propose now to turn to consider them on their own merits.

CHAPTER VII

METAPHYSICAL RESPIRATION

I BEGIN with a point that at first sight may seem remote from our main concern. It is noteworthy that when the artist undertakes to depict a state of mind, he is more likely to succeed by the indirect than by the direct method. A friend of mine tells me that the most moving representation of fear he ever saw was a picture of a man looking over his shoulder and running away as hard as he could from something—*that lay outside the frame of the picture*. What happens, I suppose, in such a case, is that the observer projects himself imaginatively into the place of the figure in the picture and sends his mind out toward that unknown shape of terror. Fear is not described directly; it is *evoked* by giving the observer something to be afraid of. In actual life intense emotions have a way of seizing upon some apparently trivial object or circumstance—"a fancy from a flower-bell"—which becomes, as it were, emotionally charged and afterward serves in recollection as a symbol potent to call up the original emotion. Poets know that the most effective way of conveying such emotion is not to attempt a direct psychological description of it, but to focus attention on the symbol.

I may take another illustration from contemporary literary fashion. I refer to what seems to me the failure of the introspectionist school of writers. They set out to explore the "inner world" of the mind. They wish to describe "the stream of consciousness" just as it flows, with its quiet reaches, its rapids, its eddies, its broken lights. Yet our general impression is that of something muddy and confused, an avalanche of shale and loose gravel, rather than a stream, without banks and without direction. Now perhaps the mind *is* something like this, though it is, I believe, the rigors of theory rather than the compulsions of observation that would lead us to think so. But the question I would ask is, Does anyone recognize these descriptions, however ingenious and subtle, as descriptions of mental life? This is what the life of the mind may *look like* to some novelist who is determined at all costs to be psychological, but is this what it *feels like* to be a mind? For myself, I can only answer, No. To an observer the mind may look like a kaleidoscope in perpetual motion, but I, as mind, am not *observing* the kaleidoscope, I *am* the kaleidoscope. It is that sense of what it means to be a kaleidoscope which is not conveyed by the now popular method of giving elaborate descriptions of the kaleidoscope.

I pass to an example that may be more generally appreciated. Philosophy and common sense are both familiar with the so-called paradox of Hedonism: to aim at pleasure directly is to miss it: the pursuit of pleasure in the abstract is self-defeating. The explanation, I suppose, is this. Pleasure is proportionate to the keenness of desire. If your desires (for objects other than pleasure) are vigorous, then you will derive pleasure from their satisfaction. What this means is that pleasure is a by-product of success or of absorption in some activity. Therefore, in order to get pleasure, we should not aim at it directly—that is, as "a state of consciousness," we should try to discover something which can command and absorb our interest. The direction of the mind should be outward, not inward.

The error of Hedonism is the error of sentimentalism everywhere—the belief that certain states of mind or certain attitudes are valuable for themselves. *Humility,* for example, has often been thus prized. But what the self-conscious cultivation of humility for its own sake produces is a false and detestable substitute for the real thing. The truly humble are those whom something has humbled. *Serenity* is a good thing, and if a man choose to secure it by mental calisthenics rather than by twenty grains of aspirin a day, that is his own business. But what one finds slightly ridiculous in the practitioners of the first kind is the notion that there is some moral or spiritual excellence about *their* serenity. For if all you want is to *feel* a certain way, what difference does it make whether you breathe deeply or take aspirin? Both are drugs; yet no one, so far as I know, has yet felt justified in becoming lyrical over the peace of aspirin that passeth all understanding. The fact is that we do not trust the serenity produced by drugs. It is not the real thing. Once again, those who are truly serene are those who have found something to be serene about.

In all these illustrations I have been trying to show that preoccupation with one's inner attitudes, the attempt of the mind to work upon itself—subjectivism in practice—produces sentimentalism and unreality; that the emotional health of the mind depends on its maintenance of the outward direction of regard. I have been, in short, concerned with pointing out the mind's need for *metaphysical respiration*. Let me proceed to exhibit this need in its practical aspect.

I shall begin by calling up the picture of some sensitive mind of our own time who stands dismayed at the account of the universe which science seems to present to him. It is not the inconceivable vastness of the cosmos which overwhelms him, nor yet its bewildering complexity, not the infinite of the great nor the infinite of the little—though these are forced upon his imagination, and they are staggering enough. No, his sensations are rather those of Pascal: "Le silence éternel de ces espaces infinis m'effraie." It is the silence, the apparent utter *indifference* of Nature, that he finds intolerable. What science seems to have done in rendering Nature impersonal is to have deprived the world of all drama, as of so much sheer mythology. The universe that is left has no history: it is, so far as one can see, a perpetual making and remaking, without reason, without purpose, without meaning. ("Time is a child playing at draughts; the kingdom is a child's.") In this vast impersonal void, the life of man, with his ideals and aspirations, seems but a point of light which flickers mysteriously for a moment and then yields to the dark. How, in such a scheme, is man to retain his self-respect or even his sanity? How can the mind stand erect in this world? Many different answers have been given to this question, many different attitudes proposed as proper to the situation. There is one in particular which in one form or another has made a strong appeal to our time: I mean the policy of heroic defiance. Man refuses to haul down the flag of humanity merely because the battle seems hopeless. He summons all his powers of resolution and self-confidence and hurls his defiance at a hostile universe. And, as we watch him do so, we seem to see the resurrection of that faith which had died.

. . . "What *art* thou afraid of? Wherefore, like a coward dost thou forever pip and whimper, and go cowering and trembling? Despicable biped! what is the sum-total of the worst that lies before thee? Death? Well, Death; and say the pangs of Tophet too, and all that the Devil and Man may, will or can do against thee! Hast thou not a heart; canst thou not suffer whatsoever it be; and, as a Child of Freedom, though outcast, trample Tophet itself under thy feet, while it consumes thee? Let it come, then; I will meet it and defy it!" And as I so thought, there rushed like a stream of fire over my whole soul; and I shook base Fear away from me forever. I was strong, of unknown strength; a spirit, almost a god. Ever from that time, the temper of my misery was changed: not Fear or whining Sorrow was it, but Indignation and grim fire-eyed Defiance.

Thus had the Everlasting No (*das ewige Nein*) pealed authoritatively through all the recesses of my Being, of my Me; and then was it that my whole Me stood up, in native God-created majesty, and with emphasis recorded its Protest. Such a Protest, the most important transaction in Life, may that same Indignation and Defiance, in a psychological point of view, be fitly called. The Everlasting No had said: "Behold, thou art fatherless, outcast, and the Universe is mine (the Devil's)"; to which my whole Me now made answer: "*I* am not thine, but Free, and forever hate thee!"*

In moods of weariness or doubt all this may seem to us but an elaborate self-deception, as though man could discover God by raising his voice; as though, in a void, a shout could be more effective than a whisper. "Ah, no," we say sadly; " 'I too know all the tunes that philosophers whistle to themselves to keep up their courage when they pass a cemetery.' " This is perhaps not wholly just, for, after all, Prometheus is a genuinely tragic figure. So is Childe Roland. And yet some justice there is in the compressed lips of the skeptic. For consider. A moment ago I used the expression "a *hostile* universe." (Inappropriately, but designedly.) But the horror of the so-called scientific nightmare is that the universe is not hostile: it is *indifferent*. Hostility a man can do with. Give him an adversary and he can stand up. For the adversary can at least *hear* his defiance. But if all one has to confront is *the silence* of these infinite spaces, then even one's heroism is empty histrionics and has only the force of a pathetic gesture.

We do wrong, therefore, to believe that defiance can, as it were, create God: God must first be there to hear our defiance if it is to have any significance. Even your passionate atheist unconsciously addresses himself to the God he has dethroned, to the God who can still hear

---

* In philosophical form I suppose the major source of the doctrine is to be found in Fichte's doctrine of the will as the creator of the universe, that doctrine in which he found escape from the two evil dreams—Subjectivism and Indifferentism.

him. In the last resort man cannot live merely by protest and will-to-believe; he cannot subsist indefinitely on his own moral tissue. The claims of human dignity and human sanity are not to be satisfied that way. If man is to find himself he must first find in the world outside some power that is either friend or foe.

Let us try to be less vague about this process called "finding oneself." What I am groping after, I suppose, is the discovery of the ultimate sources of self-respect. The commonest ground for self-respect is, perhaps, the assurance that one has been "up against" some job of work, and has come through it successfully. One has met and satisfied a demand. There are periods of slack tide in every life, long stretches of routine or of comfort when no special effort is required of us, no summoning of our powers, no critical decisions. There is nothing *at stake* in the day's work. If at such times we contrast our existence with the lives of those who have to assume a burden of responsibility, to endure hardship, or to face danger, the contrast goes all against us. It is not so much that we want to live intensely, or that some strain of the Spartan or of the ascetic in us calls out for "a little wintry negativity," as that we feel the easy-going life to be unreal. It is flabby, it lacks fiber. The judgment shows that we have lost our self-respect, and we have lost it because we are not matched with any opponent. There is no job, no commitment, no obligation that presents us with the tonic necessity of a decision between yes and no. "I don't like work, no man does," says one of Conrad's characters. "But I like what is in the work, the chance to find yourself, your own reality, for yourself, not for others—what no other man can ever know."

Now even if we leave our upholstered security and meet and pass the test of some job well done, of loyal service in a difficult enterprise, we may still fall short of the kind of assurance we are seeking. The normal standards by which we judge our success and by which we maintain our self-respect are, after all, not ultimate. No man, however well earned his success, can have been so insensitive as not to feel sometimes that there was something accidental, arbitrary, and precarious about it. He whom the world praises may be inwardly conscious of failure. Some more radical test is still to seek. Perhaps that is why we pay our tribute, openly or in secret, to the achievement of the pioneer, the sea captain, the mountain climber. These men have measured themselves against nature and have not been found wanting. And nature is the sort of ultimate for which we hunger.

Yet there is, I think, a more searching test even than that of nature, and religion holds its secret. There appears from time to time in the history of religion the idea of God as the adversary of man. You find it in the concept of the wrath of God, in the "consuming flame of divine love" of which the mystics speak. It is eloquent in the speech of the Lord to Job from the whirlwind. It has received memorable treatment in Francis Thompson's poem "The Hound of Heaven." What is finally valid in this conception is the thought that the divine scrutiny is inescapable and that there is no salvation for the soul that will not stand and turn and face that scrutiny. In the presence of God the soul stands stripped of all pretension, of all artificial merit, of all self-respect that is derived from merely human approval. God is the final judge, the ultimate test: before him one is thrown back upon whatever literal substance one has. Here is the means for the self to discover what it ultimately *amounts to*.

This fundamental need for a self-respect which rests upon self-knowledge is something that is frustrated by any subjectivist philosophy. Subjectivism forgets that man needs some Ultimate Other-than-Man against which he may measure himself; it fails to see that only the most outer can satisfy the most inner. It is because of this threat to our integrity that we fear it and seek to discredit it.

I have now examined various current solutions of the problem of religious knowledge and have rejected them. I have not proposed any theory of my own; and indeed I am not yet ready to offer a theory as definite as any of those I have analyzed. Yet, even so far, I do not think that our results need be called negative. What I have just said about subjectivism summarizes what in my own mind is the most important conclusion from our survey. My fundamental contention throughout has been that the claim of religion to convey insight about the real world may not be denied. In spite of Santayana's assertion that we should never ask of a religion whether it is true or false, but only whether it is useful or appropriate or beautiful or interesting, I am still convinced that the question of truth or falsehood is primary and inescapable. The metaphysical pretensions of religion are the most important thing about it. We cannot reduce the drama of the religious life to a mere record of mental conflict, to so much natural history of the mind. Unless the issues of destiny are at stake, there is no genuine conflict and no drama. Thus I reject all attempts to hand over religion and its problems to anthropology or sociology or psychology, as though these sciences, separately or together, could provide us with a sufficient explanation or interpretation. The problems of religion are philosophical, and there is no substitute for a philosophy of religion. Whether you call this conclusion negative or positive is, after all, merely a question of terminology. No one who is aware of our present-day perplexity about the theoretical status of religion will deny that it is a conclusion which it is worth while to establish.

NOTES

CHAPTER I

1. Ezek. 2. 1.
2. Gen. 28. 16.
3. *Elementary Forms of the Religious Life,* trans. J. W. Swann, pp. 37, 38.
4. *Space, Time, and Deity,* II, 346.
5. *Ibid.,* II, 350.
6. *The Idea of the Holy,* Eng. trans., p. 28.

CHAPTER II

1. L. P. Jacks, *Religious Perplexities,* pp. 32, 33, 56, 57, 59.
2. *Confessiones,* xi, 14.
3. Galloway, *Philosophy of Religion,* p. 331.

CHAPTER III

1. *The Meaning of Christianity,* trans. Marian Evans, pp. 11, 8.
2. *Ibid.,* p. 12.
3. *Ibid.,* pp. 17, 12, 270.
4. *Ibid.,* pp. 213, 197, 204.
5. *Ibid.,* p. 184.
6. *Ibid.,* pp. 123, 125.
7. *Ibid.,* p. 103.
8. *Ibid.,* pp. 104, 105.
9. *Ibid.,* pp. 109, 110.
10. *Ibid.,* p. 214.
11. *Ibid.,* p. 200.
12. *Ibid.,* p. 200.
13. *Ibid.,* p. 10.

CHAPTER IV

1. *Hist. of European Morals,* I, 57.
2. Aldous Huxley, *Antic Hay,* p. 8.
3. Santayana, *Reason in Religion,* p. 23.
4. *Esquisse d'une philosophie de la religion* (3d ed.), p. 88.
5. *Ibid.,* Bk. I, chaps. ii and iii, esp. pp. 63–69, 87–88.
6. *Pensées,* 347.

7. *Ibid.*, 278.
8. *Ibid.*, 485.
9. *Ibid.*, 487, 488.
10. *Ibid.*, 230.
11. Sabatier, *op. cit.*, p. 100.
12. *Ibid.*, p. 376.
13. *Ibid.*, pp. 267–268. Cf. p. 379.
14. *Ibid.*, p. 390.
15. Santayana, *Reason in Religion*, p. 98.
16. *Ibid.*, pp. 168–169.
17. *Poetry and Religion*, p. 19.
18. *Reason in Religion*, pp. 45, 46.
19. *Poetry and Religion*, pp. 108–109.
20. *Ibid.*, p. 8.
21. *Reason in Religion*, pp. 14, 98, 157.
22. *Ibid.*, p. 157.
23. *Ibid.*, p. 43.
24. *A Preface to Morals*, p. 36.

CHAPTER V

1. Jevons, *Introduction to the Study of Religion*, p. 25. This covers truly the "negative aspect of the supernatural."
2. E. S. Ames, *Religion*, p. v.
3. *Ibid.*, p. 132.
4. *Elementary Forms of the Religious Life*, Eng. trans., p. 206.
5. *Ibid.*, p. 229.
6. *Ibid.*, p. 206.
7. *Ibid.*, p. 225.
8. *Ibid.*, p. 207.
9. *Ibid.*, pp. 207, 208.
10. *Ibid.*, p. 209.
11. *Ibid.*, p. 211.
12. *Ibid.*, p. 225.
13. *Ibid.*, p. 212.
14. *Ibid.*, p. 213.
15. *Ibid.*, p. 212; cf. pp. 229, 422.
16. *Ibid.*, p. 204; cf. pp. 23–42, esp. p. 42.
17. *Ibid.*, p. 212.
18. *Ibid.*, p. 420.
19. *Ibid.*, p. 422.
20. *Ibid.*
21. *Ibid.*
22. *Varieties*, p. 188.
23. *Elementary Forms, etc.*, p. 423.
24. *Ibid.*
25. *Ibid.*, p. 422. Italics mine.

26. *My Neighbor the Universe*, pp. 77 ff.
27. *Elementary Forms, etc.*, p. 2 ; cf. pp. 59, 417, 437.
28. *Ibid.*, p. 206.
29. *Ibid.*
30. *Ibid.*, p. 10.
31. *Ibid.*, pp. 225–226.
32. *Ibid.*, p. 231.
33. *Ibid.*, p. 229 ; cf. pp. 323, 422.
34. *Ibid.*, p. 19, n. 1 ; cf. pp. 437, 438.
35. *Ibid.*, p. 19, esp. n. 2.
36. C. C. J. Webb, *Group Theories of Religion*, p. 163.

CHAPTER VI

1. *Introd. to Psychoanalysis*, p. 256.
2. *Ibid.*, p. 257.
3. Hocking, *Meaning of God*, Explanatory Notes and Essays, 1.

INDEX